PRAISE FOR
MAGNIFY YOUR MAGNIFICENCE

"Between birth and death, how shall we choose to live? In her book, Marisa Ferrera shares profound messages from Spirit that lets us know we are not alone and we have everything within us to create an extraordinary life. Inspiring and empowering!"

~ **Eva Gregory**, author of *The Feel Good Guide to Prosperity* and *Life Lessons for Mastering the Law of Attraction* co-authored with Jack Canfield and Mark Victor Hansen
EvaGregory.com, San Francisco, CA

****

"Reading Magnify Your Magnificence was like reconnecting with my soul! I heard the voice of Spirit speaking through the pages to my heart as I read the prologue: Changing Times. This information isn't new to me but it was so refreshing to be reminded in the tone of unconditional love pouring through each message. It all resonated so powerfully and as I read on I felt inspired to keep reading! If you've been searching for answers spiritually, if you've been asking questions about your true nature, if you want to connect with your life's mission... If you are curious to find out why you are here on the planet at this time and how you can experience more joy and peace in your life, if you yearn to experience your divine essence, then this book is for you! I highly recommend it!"

~ **Lorna Blake**, International Life Coach for Women Entrepreneurs and Professionals
LornaBlake.com

****

"While I started reading the book, the question, 'Why hold on to what no longer serves you?' struck me deep in my soul! It was like spirit talking to me from another source, this book...to reach me in another way! The messages and words written down in this book will uplift and help many people."

~ **Claudia V**, Netherlands

****

"It is a book you will refer to over and over and over again. Whether you read it straight through or whether you pick it up in times of frustration seeking help, it is a book you will come back to many times."

~ **Rev. Anne Presuel**,
Your 6th Sense Guide to a 6-Figure Business
DivinelyIntuitiveBusiness.com

****

"When I read Marisa's book I felt instantly free, and experienced joyous relief wash over me. This is a palpable reminder how great it feels to be the REAL me. The words that came through Marisa and spilled into her book breathed life into my soul and woke me up to the vastness of who I am and what I am innately capable of. Thank you SO much Marisa, for being the messenger of these honest, life-changing words. What a gift! With Gratitude and Admiration"

~ **Hilary**, Toronto, Canada

****

"Marisa, I just read the first message in your book and I felt the entire message deep inside of me. The words are so powerful."

~ **Marina**, Toronto, Canada

****

"I just finished reading a few of the messages from Spirit and I wanted to say Thank You! I did the exercises and it gave me some clarity. When I did the 'if you could snap your fingers' and took the time to really look at it right then...well becoming AWARE of those subterranean thoughts felt great. I think your story is amazing! Your messages are wonderful and affirming."

~ **Christine**, Writer, Ely, MN

****

"Thank you will never be enough. I can't explain how reading your book made me feel but I do know that it struck a cord with me in a way I've never felt before and I released a whole pile of 'garbage.' You are an incredible source of inspiration."

~ **Leslie**, Teacher, Ontario Canada

****

"Tonight I am saying the 'good' qualities about myself with much more conviction. Your messages are a true inspiration. Thank you so much for sharing them. I think I will make it a point to reread them at least weekly."

~ **Linda**, Nurse Practitioner, Harrisburg, PA

MAGNIFY
YOUR
MAGNIFICENCE

Your Pathway to the Life &
Relationships You Truly Desire

"Inspiring and Empowering!"

MAGNIFY YOUR MAGNIFICENCE

Your Pathway to the Life & Relationships You Truly Desire

Includes Simple-to-Follow Exercises

Marisa Ferrera

GLOBAL WELLNESS MEDIA
STRATEGIC EDGE INNOVATIONS PUBLISHING
LOS ANGELES · TORONTO

Copyright

Magnify Your Magnificence

Your Pathway to the Life & Relationships You Truly Desire

By Marisa Ferrera

MarisaFerrera.com

Website:

MagnifyYourMagnificence.com

Publisher

GLOBAL WELLNESS MEDIA

Strategic Edge Innovations Publishing
340 S Lemon Ave #2027
Walnut, California 91789-2706
(866) 467-9090

StrategicEdgeInnovations.com

Book Design and Cover
Eric D. Groleau — EricDGroleau.com

SPECIAL BONUS

**As a special thanks for purchasing this book,
I am offering you the following bonus**:

Each message you are about to read is accompanied by a powerful exercise to support you in integrating the message. You may find yourself drawn to repeating some of the exercises. To make it more convenient for you, I created a separate guide containing only the exercises, presented in a step-by-step format.

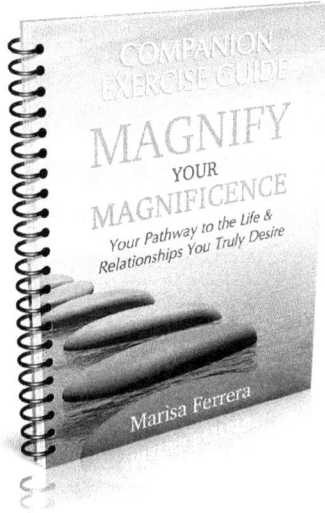

In addition to the bonus mentioned above,
I also have a surprise gift for you.

Claim Your Bonus Gifts Today!

MarisaFerrera.com/mymbonus

CONTENTS

Acknowledgements...xvii

Foreword xxi

Preface..xxiii

Prologue xxvix

Message #1: Are You Ready? 1

Message #2: Looking Within 3

Message #3: Transforming Negative Self-Talk 7

Message #4: Who Am I?...13

Message #5: Who do You Admire?.................................17

Message #6: What's Stopping You?...............................21

Message #7: Awareness, Will & Intention 25

Message #8: The Power of Gratitude.............................29

Message #9: Releasing Past Wounds 33

Message #10: Celebrate Your Accomplishments............39

Message #11: What Are You Afraid Of?.........................45

Message #12: A Time to Reflect 47

Message #13: What do You Choose to Believe? 51

Message #14: The Power of Thought 57

Message #15: You Are Never Alone 61

Message #16: Going Deeper 65

Message #17: The Importance of Self-Love...................69

CONTENTS

Message #18: Whose Voice Are You Listening To? 73

Message #19: Acknowledge Each Step 77

Message #20: Be Authentic 81

Message #21: Releasing Limiting Thoughts & Beliefs 85

Message #22: Put an End to Struggle 87

Message #23: Surrender & Trust 91

Message #24: Your True Life Purpose..95

Message #25: Embracing Your Ego...99

Message #26: Prison or Freedom...You Hold the Key.................. 103

Message #27: Stepping Out From the Crowd............................... 107

Message #28: Do You Believe in "Happily Ever After?" 113

Epilogue: The World Awaits You.. 115

About the Author.. 117

Connect with Marisa 118

Special Bonus.. 119

ACKNOWLEDGEMENTS

I first wish to acknowledge and thank the unseen, Spiritual Beings who answered my plea for direction about how I could best be of service to others and who entrusted me to record and share these profound messages with the world.

Next, I want to thank my husband Randie whose ongoing love and support gave me the confidence and courage to publicly share these messages with those who are ready to embrace them. I am so grateful for the magnificent life and relationship that we've created together and that is a demonstration to others that it IS possible to create a life and a relationship that you absolutely LOVE!

I also wish to thank my mother for always believing in me and encouraging me to follow my heart and to trust my inner guidance.

Many thanks to my dear friend and publisher Eric D. Groleau, who not only designed the cover for this book, but was always ready to lend a helping hand, providing me with technical support whenever I needed it and answering my endless questions about how to format the book properly. I would have never been able to publish this book without his expertise and guidance.

Words cannot express my gratitude to Elizabeth Jackson for proofreading this book and for always being there to provide constructive feedback, support and encouragement.

Lastly, I want to thank Rev. Anne Presuel for writing the foreword for the book and for capturing the essence of the messages with such clarity and beauty.

With my Deepest Love and Appreciation,

Marisa

I dedicate this book to you, the reader,

for your willingness and courage

to step onto a new and unfamiliar path

that will lead you to all your heart's desires.

FOREWORD

I love books that, when I'm having a challenge, I can open up and find an immediate answer. Not an answer that is vague, but one that I can sink my teeth into and then apply in my life. One that offers me a way to look at my challenge differently. Elevated. Through the eyes of the Divine.

This is one of those books.

It is a book you will refer to over and over and over again. Whether you read it straight through or whether you pick it up in times of frustration seeking help, it is a book you will come back to many times.

I call them my wisdom books. More than that, I call them my friends. Friends I turn to when I need help. Friends I look to when I need inspiration. Friends I turn to when I need guidance.

When Marisa asked me to write the foreword to Magnify Your Magnificence, I was honored. When I began to read it, I was impressed. As I continued to read it, I was hooked. From the first chapter's invitation, I knew it was special. It invited me to step into a world of deeper connection with Marisa and her powerful guides:

"Open the door to your soul's calling and you will be guided toward your destiny...one step at a time."

Channeling the energies of higher beings is a gift. It is also a skill. To be able to channel information from higher sources AND make it tangible requires that the channeler be profoundly grounded. Marisa is exactly that.

Many times channeled information requires us to sit with the guidance and mull over its message. I don't know about you, but that becomes less and less fun as I get older and older. Often, when I read channeled messages I want to yell, "Just say it so I can understand it, please!" Not so here.

Magnify Your Magnificence offers solid information. It offers solid guidance. You won't have to get together with a group to discuss what the possible meanings are. The messages are clear. And for me, that clarity is everything.

Each of the 28 messages offers not only a bit of "quickie" guidance (for those emergency, I-gotta-have-an-answer-NOW moments), but also deep lessons with step-by-step guidance on how to implement the lessons. You will not be left out in the cold wondering what the heck you are supposed to do now.

So, grab a cup of coffee (or tea), curl up in your favorite chair and start reading. You'll love the guidance. See for yourself: ask a question before you begin, because you'll definitely get an answer.

Divine Hugs,

Rev. Anne Presuel
Your 6th Sense Guide to a 6-Figure Business
DivinelyIntuitiveBusiness.com

PREFACE

Like many others, I've been on a conscious spiritual journey for many years. I was born and raised in a Roman Catholic family, explored other religions in my late 20s and 30s, studied *"A Course in Miracles"* and later became a practicing and active member of a metaphysical church. Eventually, I came to the place where I am now, believing there is a higher power that some call God, some call Source or Universal Energy and, regardless of what we call it, we can rely on this power that is within and around us at all times. I also believe we each have angels, guides and other spiritual beings who are ready to assist us at any time. All we have to do is call on them.

For as long as I can remember my passion has been to bring out the best in myself and others by uncovering the truth about who we are. By authentically sharing our unique gifts and talents with others, I believe we can create a world that better serves us all. I originally expressed my passion as a preschool and elementary school teacher, doing my best to support children in developing high levels of self-esteem and self-confidence by recognizing their greatness.

After becoming disenchanted by the public school system, which was more interested in conformity than encouraging children to BE themselves, I started my own holistic elementary school working with children who fell through the cracks in the system. I believed this was my life mission and went through some dark times as it became apparent that the school would not survive financially and I had to close it down. Even though the school no longer exists, I feel blessed to have been given the opportunity to witness the transformation of many children as they began to believe in themselves and their abilities once again.

For years after closing down the school I drifted, uncertain about what was next for me on my life journey. Since my husband and I decided we wanted to live abroad, I wanted to create a business that would give me the freedom to serve others from anywhere in the world. After several years and spending thousands of dollars on programs and workshops focused on how to build a successful business online, I was feeling frustrated, discouraged and uncertain about what direction to take in my life. I knew I wanted to share my gifts and talents in a way that would have a positive impact on the lives of others, but I didn't know how to do this. In spite of all the programs I invested in, I was going in circles and just couldn't figure out what to focus on and how to best move forward.

It was at that time that I stopped in my tracks and made a conscious decision to let go of trying to figure it all out and I surrendered. I asked God, my Higher Self, guides and angels, to show me what direction to take. I made it clear that I was not going to take another step until I felt guided to do so. Struggling and searching for me was over!

Within a few days of making this declaration, I started receiving messages in the middle of the night that I recorded on my computer. On the first morning, May 31, 2013, I was awakened at 3:33 am. I felt wide awake and compelled to get up, turn on my computer and write. I began by writing the following journal entry:

Okay, here I am. It's now 3:41 a.m. and I've been awakened, and I felt called to get up and turn on my computer. I am ready! I know I am being called to serve on a higher level and to leave behind all that has happened in the past. It is time to step up and give what I am here to give to the world. What that is, will be revealed to me in due time. For now, I must wait and trust and just BE.

"Never let the opinions of others determine your reality." I first heard this many years ago when listening to a talk by Les Brown, an internationally recognized motivational speaker, and these words have never left me. How often do we do just that? Allow the words of others to pierce our souls, to tell us who we are? When will we awaken

to the Truth of who we are...Magnificent Beings of Light, here to call forth within ourselves the beauty of who we are and to share this with the World? The world needs each of us, each and every one of us, to shine our Light, to lift us out of the darkness that has befallen us for what seems to be eternity.

When will we remember who we are? The time is NOW. The planet needs us...all of us. We have all chosen to be here at this time to co-create the New Earth.

We have been asleep long enough. It is time to get up, step up and shine our Light as brightly as we can.

How do we begin? Begin by saying, *"YES!"* Say, *"Yes, I am ready. Yes, I will awaken. Yes I will serve. Yes, I will walk toward my destiny, even if I don't know exactly what that is in this moment. Yes, I will take the first step and wait for the next step to appear. Yes, I will STOP chasing after my dreams and let them come to me. Yes, I will trust that all is well and has always been. Yes, I will BE."*

I continued writing in my journal, not realizing at first that there was a shift from my personal journal entry to a message that was coming through me. I was typing while in a meditative state and with my eyes closed and when I realized what was happening, I was startled and stopped typing in the middle of a sentence. I didn't open my eyes but sat with my fingers resting on my keyboard. At this point all kinds of thoughts started entering my mind and I was wondering what was happening and started questioning if the words were mine and, if not, where they were coming from.

I decided to test it out by not opening my eyes to read the last partial sentence that I typed. A few minutes had passed since I stopped writing and I had no idea where I left off. I took a deep breath and said something like, *"Okay, if these words are coming from Spirit I will trust that the words will continue to flow and the sentence will be completed and when I read what I recorded, I won't be able to find the place where I stopped mid-sentence." Then I said, "I am ready."*

The words continued to flow and I continued to type. When the words stopped coming I opened my eyes and read what I wrote. To my surprise and delight, I could not find the part where I stopped mid-sentence. When my husband woke up, I told him what had happened. I was a little nervous sharing the message with him and read it to him without looking up from my computer until I was finished. When I looked up, I saw tears streaming down his face and he told me he felt the message was for him. He also told me he couldn't tell where I had stopped in the middle of a sentence.

Although this gave me some confidence that something important was happening, I still went through periods of doubt from time to time, wondering if it was real or if I was making it all up. There were days and weeks when no messages came. What I found interesting was that regardless of how much time passed between receiving these messages, each one flowed into the next, providing a step-by-step guide for remembering who we ARE by first revealing who we are not. At the end of every message, I received a simple exercise to help us integrate the messages and connect more deeply to the Truth.

Since I did not go back and read past messages before recording a new one, this gave me more confidence that I wasn't making it all up and that it must have been coming from the spiritual realm. From exactly where, I wasn't sure, however, based on the wording in the messages, they appeared to be coming from a group of spiritual beings or energies and not a single entity. I wondered if they were a group of angels? Guides? Ascended Masters? It wasn't until recently that the source was revealed to me. I have been guided not to publicize the source at this time and to simply encourage you to read each message with an open mind and an open heart.

Since each message builds on the previous one, it is best to read them in order the first time through. If you wish to receive the most value from these powerful messages, I encourage you to complete each exercise that accompanies each message before moving on to the next one. If possible, record your responses in a journal so that you can refer back to them as you delve deeper and deeper into your Truth.

The remaining content of this book, including the Prologue and Epilogue are words that came through me. These messages are not only for my personal benefit but for yours as well. If you have a desire in your heart to KNOW yourself, your True self, and to learn how you can BE, DO and HAVE whatever your heart desires, then this book is for you.

I am excited about what is possible for you as you allow these words to touch your soul and transform your life.

Love & Blessings,

Marisa

PROLOGUE

CHANGING TIMES

It is everyone's desire to be at peace and yet so few in your world experience this. Why do you think this is so? Remember that the outer world is but a reflection of the inner. You are not at peace because you know deep within you that you are not living to your full potential. You know that somewhere along the way, you stopped yourself from expressing yourself authentically.

The turmoil you witness in the outer world is increasing because more and more of you are waking up and feeling the discrepancy between who you are and how you are expressing yourself. You are beginning to feel the discordant vibrations and your real Self is no longer willing to take a back seat, to sit in silence while watching yourself and your world disintegrate. Your real self knows the importance of waking up and taking a stand, not only for yourself but for all of humanity.

Ready or not, times are changing and this will be frightening for some of you. It doesn't have to be. In fact, it can be very exciting, for as all that you've known to be true is washed away, the new can emerge and take its place...a new world, a new way of being for ALL. No more hatred, no more lack, no more pain and suffering. Yes, this IS possible but not until the old is washed away...all of it.

As you begin to wash away the lies and untruths about who you are, the world itself will emerge into itself, its True self. Your world has been darkened by all the lies. It has been reflecting back the collective consciousness of its inhabitants and as each of you remembers the Truth about who you are, the world can also return to its natural and inherent Magnificence, for it will reflect this remembrance.

Your Truth has been hidden in your heart. As you begin to open your heart, you will see this Truth more and more. If you complete the exercises presented in this book, you will know that what we are saying is true, for you will begin to experience this Truth for yourself.

As the systems in your world break down to make room for the new, many will suffer a great deal, not because this is required, but because they are too attached to the old and will hold on tighter and tighter as they begin to see things collapse. It is this holding on that will cause great suffering and pain. If you are willing to let more and more go, and not be attached to anything, you will experience this transition with more ease and grace. It really is up to you.

Why hold on to what isn't working, what has never really worked? Yes, we understand that this is all you have known and there is fear of the unknown, and we are here to remind you that we DO know what is ahead and we can tell you that it is more beautiful than you can imagine in this moment. We ask that you place your trust in us and allow us to guide you each step of the way. Whenever you are faced with fear and doubt, call on us and ask for our support and we will gladly offer it to you. You must first ask before you can receive our guidance and support for it is available to you always and it is our pleasure to provide this for you.

It is time to go deeper into your true essence. You are much more than you have ever imagined. You are a co-creator with God. God lives, breathes and expands through your expression and through your creations. God and you are one being, one Light. As you expand your Light, the Light of God becomes stronger. We realize this is a difficult concept for some to grasp especially given what you have been taught.

As an infinite Being, God has no beginning and no end, just as you have no beginning and no end. We are not speaking of your physical life for this is such a small part of your existence. We are speaking of the totality of who you are beyond the earthly plane. Your time on earth is but a glimpse of all that is and for many of you this is all that you can see. There is so much more and we are here to help you to see more so that you can tap into this well of unlimited abundance at will.

Many Blessings Dear One

MESSAGE #1

ARE YOU READY?

There has never been a time on earth as precious as this one. Never before have there been so many who are willing to answer *"Yes"* to the call deep within their souls. Many of you are awakening at this time and this pleases us. We are here to help guide you along this path. You have nothing to fear. Just open yourself up to ALL possibilities. Let go of your limiting beliefs that have kept you stuck for so long. Life is not meant to be a struggle. The time for struggle is over. You are here to usher in a new reality, one that will be of service to all and one that will help light the way for others to follow.

There has never been a time when the world needed you as much as now.

You may think you are only one person, but don't forget that one plus one is more than two. You are not alone on this path. There are many who you do not see and who are here walking with you, gently nudging you forward. Listen to the small, still voice within you. Take time to BE and to stop DOING.

Yes, we know, time is such a problem for many of you. But time is an illusion, one that you created and one that you can recreate to serve you and the world. Let go of the need to DO and to achieve. Let go of the need to pursue and to prove yourself to others. There is nothing to prove. You ARE enough and have always been enough. Let go of the lies you've been told. Wake up to the Truth. The Truth is you are loved beyond measure. The Truth is you are a bright, shining Light who has dimmed or hidden yourself for fear of being seen by those who you feel are here to hurt you and put you down. It is true that for many years, shining your Light has been dangerous. For some, shining your Light has been painful.

"Where is all of this going?" you may ask. You seem to have a need to see far ahead of your journey. This is not necessary. You only need to see as far as your next step and once you arrive, you will see the next and the next. Listen...Listen...What is your heart telling you? Quieten your mind's chatter so you can hear the Truth buried deep within your heart. It's okay to let this out now.

Open the door to your soul's calling and you will be guided toward your destiny...one step at a time.

Just begin and see where this leads you. You may be surprised to find that it's not as hard as you had imagined. It is natural to you. What is hard is the way you have been living your life so far, repressing your Truth, and denying the very essence of your soul. You have chosen a very painful path. We are here to liberate you, to help set you free. You, however, must be the one to say *"Yes, I am ready. I am ready to let go of the invisible chains that have bound me."*

Your first step is to repeat the mantra: *"I AM ready. I AM ready."* You may wish to begin by closing your eyes and taking a few deep breaths to center yourself. Sit in silence for as long as you wish repeating these words. There is nothing else at this time.

MESSAGE #2

LOOKING WITHIN

A ll of you know the importance of love and yet look at your planet. Where is the love in children starving all around the world? Where is the love in women and girls being raped? Where is the love in those who have no food to feed their families, no roof to put over their heads? Your planet is filled with hate, jealously, envy and anger. Why? How did this happen? As beings of Light, how did you turn to so much darkness?

The reason is because you have forgotten who you are. You ARE love even though many of you do not live this. You are Light even though many of you choose to spread darkness.

It is not too late to shift and make the world a better place.

It is not too late to change your ways and to dig deep inside to find your Light and let it shine. Many of you have done this and many more are waking up. This is good. As you begin to awaken, you join the others who are doing the same and together your Light gets even stronger. Do not worry if you think your Light is too small because there is no such thing as being too small. Even a flicker of Light will brighten a darkened room. It doesn't take much to fill a room with Light.

Begin with yourself. Look inside and see what is there. Look inside in every corner of your being. Turn on your inner Light and it will shine outwards for others to see. Your Light can help not only yourself but those around you. You can help them find their way simply by finding your own. Focus on yourself...yes, yourself and not others. As you shift and grow, others will see and those who are ready will follow, just as you are ready or you would not be reading this. You would not even have found this book if you were not ready.

Something inside you has called you into being more open, more curious, and more aware. You listened to this small still voice, or perhaps for you it was a loud voice, the voice of cancer, the voice of pain, the voice of disease. Whatever it was that turned you inward does not matter. What matters is that you are here NOW and you are ready, ready to shift and to become your TRUE self and we are here to help you.

You are never alone and you have never been alone. When you felt alone it was because you turned your Light off. We have always been here, shining our Light for you to see, shining our Light to light your path and lighten your load. We are sorry you have chosen to suffer for so long and delighted that you are now ready to return home to your heart and soul.

Yes, it's been a long and difficult journey until now. Now you will see the road more clearly. Now you will feel your load lighten. Now you will see, perhaps for the first time, all the illusions you have allowed to stop you from living your life to the fullest. Rejoice in this new awakening! You have joined many others and now you will see them. They too have walked your earth forever, but only those who are ready can see others who carry this Light and shine it brightly.

"You were blind but now you see." Yes, Jesus' words are as true today as they were over two thousand years ago. His teachings have been sadly distorted over time but don't forget the real Jesus, the true messenger of Light. Don't discard his message because of those who distorted it. He truly was, and continues to be, one of those who can lead the way, along with many others.

"Love thy neighbor as thyself." You must love yourself before you will be able to truly love another. This is also why your world is so full

of darkness. Many of you are filled with self-hatred and feelings of unworthiness. You project all of this onto your outer world making it a dark place both inside and out.

Your outer world will not change until you change your inner world.

Yes, at times it might be scary. Just like entering a dark room and an unfamiliar place, you don't know what you will find there. But let us assure you, what you will find are all the illusions of your past, all the lies you've been told, all the stories you've told yourself and others have told you that do not serve you or them. But that is not all you will find. You will also find the Truth; the beauty of what lies within you. You will find strength, courage, determination and vision. You will find your true Self and you will be pleased. This we KNOW and soon you will know.

Take one step at a time as you look within. Today, begin by taking a few moments to sit quietly, close your eyes, take a few deep breaths and take a peek at what is in your mind and heart. Allow yourself to simply notice your thoughts. Don't try to make your thoughts go away. Accept them and love them. Simply notice what is there. They serve a purpose. If you find it helpful, take time to write about your thoughts and whatever else pops up for you. Remember there are no good or bad thoughts. They are simply thoughts. When you feel complete, thank your thoughts for revealing themselves to you. Thank them for showing you what is within you at this time. They will lead you to your Truth.

TRANSFORMING NEGATIVE SELF-TALK

L isten. Listen to what is all around you. What do you hear? Does what you hear please you or does it disturb you? Now, listen to your thoughts. Do your thoughts please you or do they disturb you?

When you are listening to the radio and you don't like what is playing, what do you do? Do you continue to listen and get more and more aggravated, complaining about the song and wishing it was over so you wouldn't have to listen to it anymore? No, you reach over and either turn it off or change the channel. How difficult is it for you to do this? What results do you experience?

Why is it then, that when you do not like the thoughts that keep roaming around in your head, you choose to continue to listen to them over and over again, driving you to madness?

Just as you have the power to change the channel on a radio station, you also have the power to change the channel in your mind.

You do not have to listen to thoughts that disturb you, thoughts that bring you down, thoughts that tell you things that aren't even true. You have the power to change the channel and listen to more beautiful thoughts, thoughts that empower you, thoughts that inspire you, thoughts that reveal the Truth.

You may think this is difficult and this too is a thought. Take out a piece of paper or a notepad. Write down the words, *"I am stupid."* Underneath write the words, *"I am smart."* If, for some reason you are unable to write, think these two statements in your mind. Could you do it? Of course you could. Why? Because you CHOSE to. If you didn't do it, why is that? It is for the same reason: because you CHOSE not to do it.

It is the same with the thoughts in your mind. You can choose to continue to listen to them and let them control your life, or you can CHOOSE to take control of your thoughts and therefore, be more in control of your life. This is not to say that random thoughts will not continue to pop into your mind.

***The more you choose which thoughts to hold
on to and which ones to stop listening to,
the happier and more fulfilled you will be.***

So, what do you do when you find yourself thinking negative thoughts? You make a choice to think a different thought that better serves you or better serves others. For example, let's say you keep thinking you are a failure. You can, of course, come up with all kinds of evidence to prove that you are a failure. How does this impact your life when you choose to focus on this? Does it make you feel good? Does it inspire you to move forward? Chances are, telling yourself over and over that you are a failure or that you are not good enough or that you are not attractive enough or that you are not smart enough, results in more and more negative feelings and therefore negative experiences in your life.

Only you can put a stop to this. It will not matter how many times others tell you that you are smart or attractive or lovable, if you do not tell yourself this, your life will not change. YOU must believe the Truth about who you are.

You may be thinking, *"But it is true that I'm a failure. I can't find a decent job or I lost my business."* You might be thinking *"But it's true that I'm not lovable. I've been alone for so many years and nobody wants me."*

No matter what you think about yourself or your abilities in this moment, if it is not filling your heart with joy, it is a lie, no matter how much evidence you can produce to prove otherwise.

Even if you don't believe us, what do you have to lose to give this a chance? You are reading this book because you have a desire to change, to grow, to evolve, to experience more of what you want and less of what you don't want. So take this opportunity to move in a new direction, one that will lead you to your Truth, to more peace, happiness, abundance and joy.

Today, take some time to notice what you are thinking. What are you saying to yourself throughout the day? If you can take a few moments now to write down some of your negative self talk, that would be great.

Here is a list to get you started. Choose the ones that you believe to be true about yourself or that you've told yourself or others from time to time and add any that are missing from the list.

* I am stupid.

* I am ugly.

* I can't do anything right.

* I am a failure.

* I am poor.

* I am unlovable.

* I am not good enough.

* I am not smart enough

* I am not _____ enough.

* I can't _____.

How do you feel when you think these thoughts? Are you uplifted and ready to take on anything? Chances are you feel down or depressed or possibly sad or angry.

Now, next to each negative thought, write down the opposite.

* I am smart.

* I am beautiful.

* I can make anything work.

* I am successful.

* I am rich.

* I am lovable.

* I am enough.

* I am very smart.

* I am _____.

* I can _____.

Sometimes negative self-talk may sound like this...

* I don't have enough time.

* I don't deserve to be wealthy.

* I'm overwhelmed.

* I'll never figure out how to_____.

Here are some suggestions for turning these negative thoughts into more powerful thoughts.

* Time is an illusion and is on my side. I have all the time in the world.

* Abundance is my natural birthright and everything comes to me easily and effortlessly.

* I am confident in my ability to move through each moment with comfort and ease.

* I am capable of learning ANYTHING I choose and of being successful at it.

How do the positive statements make you feel? Perhaps you can't yet feel the Truth of these statements. Perhaps these statements bring up more thoughts that say, *"But this isn't true."* If this is the case, and even if it isn't, take one of the positive statements and write it down on a small card or note. Read it from time to time throughout the day and pretend it is true. Pretend you are an actor in a movie and you are required to play the part of someone who is very smart, or successful or attractive and you need to practice this role before you can shoot the movie.

Practice feeling the words, the Truth of the words, so that you can play the part very well. Keep practicing this role until you become it. You can play with the other positive statements and incorporate them into your role as well. Keep practicing until it becomes effortless and you become the smart, successful, lovable person that you are.

You may think this is silly and it can't really work. Do you know that you have already been doing this all your life...unconsciously? Did you know that you took on the roles of stupid, or ugly, or unsuccessful or _____?

Did you know you have been acting a role all your life without even knowing it?

The problem is that you did not consciously choose the role you wanted to play. You accepted the role that others gave you. You don't have to act out this role any longer if it does not serve you. You can act out any role you choose. You can rewrite the script of your life and play ANY role. We will talk more about this later.

For now, it is enough to pay attention to your negative self-talk and do your best to change it into something positive as soon as you become aware of it. You can also ask a friend or loved one to help you with this. You can give them permission to remind you, or point out to you, any time you say something negative about yourself so that you can shift the thought in the moment.

We promise you this. If you are willing to take on the role of who you want to be, you will discover that this is who you have always been. You put your true Self aside when you took on the roles that have been given to you. Now you can go back to being YOU!

MESSAGE #4

WHO AM I?

Discovering your life purpose...isn't that what you have been seeking? Why, you may ask, is it so difficult to know what it is? There are many books that have been written about this, and many more will be written. The fact is, however, it will not matter how many books you read because your true purpose will not be revealed to you until you are ready. You must desire to know this Truth from a place of contributing to the world, not from a place of serving only yourself. You must sincerely want to be of service to others.

By giving to others from your heart, you give to yourself as well.

When you give to others from your head, from a place of obligation, you take away from yourself and in turn begin to resent others. This does not fill you up, but depletes you. When you give to others from a place of lack, you will feel burdened. When you give from a place of abundance, you will feel joy and the more you give, the more you have to give. You will never feel depleted.

Many of you have been giving to others in an attempt to fill something within yourself that is lacking. You give to others what you want for yourself and, in doing so, others may or may not benefit and although you may feel some level of fulfillment, you continue to feel you are not enough and what you are contributing is not enough. You continue to strive and to give until your well runs dry and you have nothing left to give. You are then left with feeling disappointed and discouraged, wondering why you have such difficulty manifesting what you desire.

The reason is this. You have not yet filled yourself up and unconsciously are giving to others with the false belief that this will make you whole, will make you feel complete, will make you feel worthy.

Before you can truly give to others,
you must give to yourself.

Before you can discover your true purpose, you must first discover your true Self. This is not to say that others will not benefit from your contributions. They will. However, you will not be able to sustain it for long for it will deplete you.

For now, let go of your need to know why you are here and focus instead on yourself and discovering the Truth about who you are. Today, ask yourself...

"Who am I?"

Take some time to reflect on this question and if possible, record your responses to this question. Keep asking the same question, *"Who am I?"* Notice whatever pops in your mind, no matter what it is. If you choose to write down your automatic responses, make sure to record EVERY answer that comes to you without editing it in any way.

Next, look at each response and ask yourself, *"Is this the Truth about who I Am or is this what I have come to believe about who I am because of my conditioning and my life experiences?"* The more honest you can be when completing this exercise, the closer you will get to the Truth.

Continue to ask yourself this question throughout the day and see if you can notice times when you tell yourself things like, *"I'm so stupid. I can't believe I did that."* Or *"I'm never going to figure this out."* These types of statements will also reveal to you who you think you are. Any time you begin a statement with *"I am"* you are declaring who you think you are. Watch for the times you say these words and if possible record what comes next.

MESSAGE #5

WHO DO YOU ADMIRE?

This is an important day. This is the day when you will begin to see who you are, not who you think you are.

Have you ever looked into the eyes of a baby? What did you see? Did you see an ugly, good-for-nothing individual who was not worthy of love? No, you saw an innocent, beautiful being with unlimited possibilities. This is you! You are that baby! You may have an adult body but it is time to bring yourself back to when you entered this world, time to go back and see yourself as an innocent child, a beautiful child with unlimited possibilities. This has always been who you are. You have simply forgotten.

You have bought into all the lies that you have been told over the years. You have made decisions for your life based on these lies and based on experiences in which you told yourself over and over again that you are not good enough, not worthy enough, not _____ enough.

You are MORE than enough. What will it take to convince you of this? What will it take for you to SEE the Truth about this? When did you decide that what others told you was the Truth and that what you held inside you was not? When will you choose to STOP and come back to You, who you truly are? Only you can do this. You suffer and wonder why. The Truth is that you suffer because you are not willing to see the Truth. Instead, you hold on tight to the lies for fear of losing yourself.

You lost yourself many years ago. You lost yourself the first time you believed that you were unlovable, or unworthy or not capable.

You lost yourself and you continue to lose more and more of yourself every day. Bit by bit you lose a piece of yourself and each time you do, you make it more difficult to KNOW yourself.

You want to believe that you have no control over your current circumstances, but this is not the Truth. You want to believe that if your external situation was different, better, all would be well with you. This is not true. It will not matter what changes on the outside of you. Yes, you may have moments of happiness and contentment but if you rely on external circumstances for your fulfillment and your peace, you will continue to suffer.

The ONLY way to experience true joy, true peace, true abundance, is to source from within.

You must look inside yourself for ALL of this and believe you already have it within you and then you will experience the Truth. Then your life will no longer be at the mercy of others or of circumstances because you will get to CHOOSE how you want to BE no matter what is going on around you.

This may seem like an impossible task and we understand this. You have spent a good part of your life looking outside yourself. You know, or think you know, how to deal with what is going on. You have developed tools and ways to cope, for the most part. These tools have served you well at times and at other times may have destroyed a part of you.

The good news is that you are capable of restoring yourself to your TRUE self, the person you came into the world as being. It does not have to take a long time, as you may now be thinking. All it takes is a commitment to allowing this Truth to reveal itself to you, one step at a time. You have already begun this process or you would not be reading these words right now. Your WILL is the first step, your willingness to shift, to see yourself differently.

18

We don't know how many times we must tell you that you are NOT who you think you are. You are NOT what or who others say you are.

You are pure Light and Joy! You are a Co-creator! You are a Bright Light! You are a Magnificent Being!

You have so much within you, but it has been hidden, buried, forgotten. Now is the time to bring yourself back to WHO YOU ARE. This is not just so that you will have a better life. It is because the world needs you to return to your Truth. The world, as you know, is in danger and humanity itself is in danger and needs every one of you to awaken in order to save yourself and your world. We do not say this to bring fear. We say it because it is the Truth and as Jesus said, *"The Truth will set you free."*

The Truth at times may seem scary, but it is the lies that are most scary; the false beliefs that you hold that are scary, for these are the things that will destroy you and your world.

Think about someone you admire. You may want to think of several people you admire. Write down or think about the qualities this person or these people have that you admire so much. Make the list of qualities as long as possible. Then read over this list.

You ARE each and every one of these qualities. The only difference between you and them is that they discovered the Truth about who they are and they allowed their Light to shine from within to brighten not only their own life but the lives of others. You are the same but you don't believe it.

Now, go back to this list of qualities you admire in others. Take each quality and say to yourself, out loud if possible, *"I am (and then name the quality)"*. It does not matter if, in this moment, you do not believe these statements are true. What matters is that you are WILLING to do this exercise to support yourself in reclaiming your true self.

19

Just as before, choose one quality and repeat the statement through the day as often as possible. Repeat this statement as an affirmation. Speak it out loud as many times as possible and with expression. Once again, act out the role of believing you possess this quality. Keep acting until you can speak these words and you no longer feel resistance. Speak these words until you not only believe them to be true but KNOW deep within you that they are true.

As you rediscover your true Self, you will begin to understand more and more what has been going on in your world for many, many years. The time has come for each of you to stand up and reclaim your power and the only way to do this is to reclaim your Self.

MESSAGE #6

WHAT'S STOPPING YOU?

Take a look at your life today. Where do you stand? Is everything how you had hoped it would be by this stage in your life? Are you living your dream life? If not, why not? What got in the way? What stopped you from living the life you always wanted to live? Your life and how you live it is your choosing. You are where you are today because of every choice you made up to this point.

So many of you are not only NOT living your dreams, but you've forgotten what your dreams are. Others know what you want to experience in life, but lament that it is not so.

When you were a child, your options were more limited. But you are no longer a child. You can no longer blame your childhood for your current circumstances. *"But, But"* you say. *"If it weren't for my childhood experiences, I wouldn't be who I am today."* Although your experiences as a child shaped who you are today and started you on your path, you are no longer limited by your past conditioning unless you choose to be.

When will you take your wounded child out of the driver's seat and put your "real" Self there?

How long will you blame your childhood for your life not working out the way you want it to? As long as you continue to blame your childhood for your current circumstances you will NEVER live your dream life. No matter where you are in your life right now, it is temporary. Every moment offers you an opportunity for change, for growth, for new possibilities. By now, most of you have heard a famous quote, *"If you keep on doing what you've always done, you'll keep on getting what you've always got."* (W.L Bateman) There are different versions of this and they all have the same meaning.

You know much more than you think about how to make changes in your life. You've even thought about them from time to time and decided it would be too difficult, or it's too late or it's best to just accept things the way they are.

It is never too late to make a shift and move in a new, more empowered direction in your life.

Accepting your current circumstances does not mean you have to continue to live them over and over again. No matter how difficult it may seem to turn your life around, to live the life you dreamed about, you CAN do this, if you want it badly enough. No, you can't change the past, so if part of your dream is about how you wished things could have been during your past years, you must accept this and let go of the disappointment or sadness of what could have been. The more you choose to continue to think about these things, the less chance you have to create the life you truly desire from this point forward.

You cannot change the past. You can only change your thoughts about it.

Today, take some time to reflect on your life, both your past and where you are right now. Look at your entire life to this point and write down all your disappointments, hurts, resentments, fears, what you think is holding you back. Write down why you believe your life isn't working or why you believe your life isn't where you want it to be.

This will take some time, so it is best to do this exercise when you can take as much time as you need or want and when you can be free from distractions and interruptions. If possible, find a place in nature and take a journal or notepad with you. It is time to release the past so that you can make room for something new.

You have allowed your past to define who you are and it is important to understand this so that you can take back your life and redesign it from a place of Truth. We will look at this in more detail later. For now it is enough to simply write down everything that you feel isn't working in your life right now and your beliefs about why you think this is so. Be honest with this. The more honest you can be about why you think you are where you are right now, the more freedom you will experience. Write down all the thoughts that come up for you as you record your hurts and disappointments, for this too will be very revealing and will help you uncover the Truth.

If emotions come up for you as you work through this exercise, allow yourself to express them and release them. Do your best not to get lost in them because this will not serve you. Remind yourself that these feelings are leaving you and making room for creating what you truly desire, making room for you to experience your True self.

You may find it helpful to repeat the words. *"I let go of this feeling of _____, and I give thanks that I am creating room for my real Self to emerge."* Bask in the Truth of these statements and then move on to your next thought or feeling until you feel complete.

If you find yourself getting lost in your emotions or feeling overwhelmed by them, you may want to consider working with a personal coach or mentor who can support you through this process. The key here is to recognize the feelings and thoughts that are holding you back, to release them and fill yourself with the excitement of redesigning your life from a place of freedom and Truth.

MESSAGE #7

AWARENESS, WILL & INTENTION

C an you remember a time when you were so happy that you felt on top of the world, or a time when you accomplished something you thought you could never do? This feeling of excitement and jubilation is your natural state of being. You came here with such anticipation, such curiosity, looking forward to all that you could create from this place of joy. What you did not realize was how hard it would be to maintain this state of joy, curiosity, and excitement in the face of obstacles and unexpected circumstances.

You forgot that you are capable of overcoming anything that crosses your path and that you have everything you need inside of you.

You forgot that your true essence, the core of who you are, IS joy, IS abundance and that all you need to do is call this forth and it will be present to you. Instead, when faced with difficulties, you shut down, pull back, lose hope. Do not blame yourself for this and do not blame others. There is no one to blame. It is simply a fact. The good news is that now that you are aware of this, you have the power to do something about it.

Awareness is the first step to transformation. Without it, you are stuck, stuck in your pain, stuck in your illusions, stuck in your limiting beliefs. This does not mean that once you are more aware, all of this will magically disappear. These untruths, lies, and limiting beliefs have been a part of you for a very long time and, although it could take but an instant for them to be removed, it is not likely that you will have the strength, the courage or the belief to let them all go at once. This is okay. Be patient with this process. It will take whatever time it needs. There is no need to hurry or to feel anxious about this.

It is important to allow this process to move through you with its own timing and rhythm. Let go of how long it *"should"* take. Let go of the need for *"it"* to be over now. The process is *"The Way."* It is the path to your transformation. It is the path to the journey back to YOU. As you walk this path, remind yourself that you are not alone.

If you are feeling stuck, afraid, or hopeless, ask for help.

You can ask your earthly friends or loved ones or your guides, angels and spirit beings who are all around you waiting to assist you. You simply need to call on them. They cannot help you unless you ask. This is the law of free Will. Believing in angels or spirit guides is not a religious thing. No one is asking you to believe in anything. What we are asking is for you to let go of what you believe to be true and be open to new possibilities. Hold on to your beliefs that serve you and let go of the rest. You do not need them. Allow yourself to be open to new possibilities of what is true. Let go of your limited thinking that things should be a certain way.

Today take some time to reflect on times in the past when you felt ALIVE, happy, excited, filled with joy, confidence...any time that you felt great. Record these events and as you remember more and more pleasant memories from your past, you can add to this list. If you have difficulty remembering times like this, ask yourself, *"What experiences would bring these feelings forward for me? What would have to happen in my life in order for me to feel abundant, joyful, excited."* If your past was so filled with pain that you can't remember even a single moment when you experienced joy or confidence or anything pleasant, do not fret about this. Simply continue to focus on what you believe would bring these feelings to you.

When you feel complete, go back and read each item on your list, one at a time, and allow yourself to feel the energy of what you are reading. Imagine that this event or situation is happening right now and relive these joyful memories. Allow yourself to be fully immersed in each experience. If you do not have any joyful memories and if you are having difficulty believing in the experiences you wish to draw to you, remember the *"acting"* you have been doing with other exercises and act as if you are living it now, role play. What is important here is for you to raise your vibration and your energy to the level of happiness, joy, love.

If you are having trouble role playing, ask your spirit guides to help you. Even if you don't believe they are really there, take the step and ask anyway and see what happens. It is through your Will and your intention that your life will change, that you will be led to your Truth.

MESSAGE #8

THE POWER OF GRATITUDE

Give thanks that you are here. Give thanks that you are alive. Give thanks that you have been led to this work that is of great importance, not only for you but for your entire planet. You have been given a gift, an opportunity to discover the Truth, the Truth about you, the Truth about others, the Truth about your planet. As you continue to learn and as you continue to work through the exercises in this book, you will continue to grow and to evolve.

Today is about gratitude. No matter what is going on in your life right now, there are many things you can be grateful for. It is up to you to be willing to see the Truth about EVERYTHING. If you choose to only focus on what is not working in your life, you will not see the beauty of what IS working. Have you ever thought that maybe some of what you feel hasn't been working in your life is a clue that can lead you to the Truth? Yes, as strange as this may sound, it is true.

You see, you have a choice to make. Now that you are becoming more aware of what is really going on within you, you can choose to continue to think in your old ways, in ways that bring you pain, doubt, and confusion, or you can change your thoughts and draw forth the experiences you truly desire. It begins with being in a state of gratitude.

Unless you can BE, and feel grateful for what you have now, for your current state of affairs and look for the blessings in everything, it will be difficult for you to attract more of what you want into your life.

A lack of gratitude stops the flow of abundance into your life. A lack of gratitude stops you from seeing who you are. A lack of gratitude stops you from truly living, from being free. It is not difficult to take on an attitude of gratitude.

It's funny how many of you set aside one day a year to give thanks. You call it, *"Thanksgiving Day"*. Why not be in a state of gratitude and give thanks every day? Can you not take a few moments every day to say thank you. Thank you for what is already present in your life, and thank you for what is on its way? Of course you can do this. It is up to you. You can take even a minute as you wake up, as you brush your teeth, as you are on your way to work. There are so many moments in the day when you can give thanks without it interfering or taking up extra time. If you begin to take opportunities to express gratitude, you will be amazed at how your life will change.

For now, it would be helpful to make a list of everything you can think of for which you can be grateful. Things like the fact that you are breathing. If you can walk, be grateful for this for there are many who can't. If you can see, be grateful for this for there are many who can't. If you can hear, be grateful for this for there are many who can't.

Simply start with *"I am grateful for..."* or *"I am thankful for..."* whichever resonates more with you. Make the list as long as possible. It does not have to include only big things, for there is no difference between what you may consider big and small. Are you grateful that the sun comes out each day, even if it is hidden by clouds? Do you have a roof over your head, food to eat or clean water to drink? As you begin to make your list, more and more will become present to you.

Take time throughout each day to give thanks. Look for opportunities that present themselves. Give thanks if someone smiles at you at the grocery store. Give thanks if you get a green light when driving. Give thanks for the beauty of the trees, flowers, birds. There is so much to be thankful for.

If it helps you, set a timer on your phone or watch so that it goes off a few times a day and when it does, take a moment to give thanks for something…anything. Allow yourself to not only say the words, but to FEEL the Truth behind them. If you can't feel thankful for being able to walk, imagine what it would be like if all of a sudden you couldn't. Sometimes when you imagine the opposite of something, you will find it easier to be thankful that it isn't so.

We cannot stress enough how important this is. The vibration of your entire being will shift as you focus on gratitude. You do not have to believe us based on these words. Practice this every day and, if you are consistent, you will experience this Truth.

.

MESSAGE #9

RELEASING PAST WOUNDS

Remember a time when you felt sad, hurt or disappointed. When you think or talk about this experience, how do you feel? Do you feel what you felt at the time it actually happened, or are you able to think and talk about it as simply a memory, with no upsetting feelings attached to it? You see, the past is over and yet for many of you, you continue to unconsciously re-live it over and over again and wonder why your life does not change or does not work.

You are who you are today, not because of the actual events that happened in your past, but because of the meaning you attached to those events.

How you experience and see yourself today is not the real you. It is the "you" that emerged from your experiences here on earth. The real you somehow got locked up inside. Your experiences, no matter what they were, served a purpose. Each experience taught you something and, depending on how you choose to look at it, it either taught you something that can serve you and others or it will cause you to hurt yourself and others.

If, for example, you interpret an experience as meaning you are not good enough, smart enough, attractive enough, and so on, do you believe these thoughts and interpretations will serve you or hurt you? Do these thoughts empower you or bring you down? It's pretty obvious, isn't it? And yet, chances are, your interpretation of past events leads you to feeling small, less than, incapable of fulfilling your dreams and unable to achieve what you desire.

There is another way to look at your experiences, to view them from your Higher Self rather than your lower self, a way to use every experience from your past as an opportunity to see the Truth and to reveal your true essence. This, for some of you may be difficult.

If you are willing to shift into a new way of thinking about your past, you will create a new way of living from this moment forward, a way that will be a true reflection of who you are and what you are truly capable of creating.

You will need to be patient with yourself as you work through painful memories from the past. You will need to be gentle with yourself. There may be memories that you have chosen not to look at for a very long time. What you may not realize is that just because you buried them, this does not mean they are not there. This does not mean they are not impacting your life in ways that you are not conscious of. By shining the Light on what you have buried within you, the Truth will be revealed and you can let go of all that is holding you back from experiencing a full and joyous life. This really is possible no matter what your life looks like today.

Once again, all that is needed to get started is your willingness to look at the Truth of the past and not what you made up about it. This is not to say you have been intentionally lying about your past experiences. What you experienced was real. It is the thoughts and beliefs you attached to them, the interpretations of them, the judgments about them that you made up, and, depending on what you made up about all of this, your experiences are either supporting you in living your life from a place of your true Self, or they are limiting you and hiding who you are.

Today you are being asked to take some time to work through one painful past memory so that you can release it and let it go. Of course, you may choose to work through as many memories as you like. What is important is that you go through each of the following steps completely with one memory before moving on to the next. We recommend that you begin with a memory that is less emotionally charged and, as you become more familiar with the exercise and how it works, choose more painful memories.

It would be helpful for you to come back to this exercise as often as possible until you feel your past experiences are no longer holding you back. You can then go through these steps any time a new experience brings up feelings of upset, sadness, anger, etc. so that you no longer bury painful experiences but deal with them in a way that sets you free.

The more honest you can be as you work through this exercise, the more liberating it will be for you. Keep in mind that this exercise is not intended to bring up emotions so that you can get stuck in them. In fact, do your best to step outside of yourself and look back as an observer, as if you are interviewing someone else and asking them these questions. It is not necessary for you to re-live these memories in order to heal from them or to let them go. What is important is to see what is there, to shed Light on what is there so that these memories no longer hold you back or limit you from being who you are, your true authentic self.

Step 1: What Actually Happened

Write down your memory in as much detail as possible. How old were you? Who else was present? What time of year was it? Where did it take place? What actually happened? What emotions did you experience when it happened...fear, anger, hurt, disappointment?

Step 2: What You Made it Mean

What were you thinking when it happened? Include any thoughts you had about yourself or any other people involved. For example, were you thinking you were bad, stupid, ugly? Were you thinking the other person was being mean or they didn't love you? Dig deep and allow all your thoughts about this experience to emerge.

When you talk about this incident and share it with others, what feelings come up for you? Do you find yourself getting angry, sad? What thoughts do you have about it today? Do you have the same thoughts and feelings as you did in the past or are they different? Again, include thoughts and feelings about yourself and others. What did you make this experience mean about you and/or others?

Step 3: Impact on Your Life

How do you think or feel this experience has impacted your life? What circumstances in your life do you tend to blame on this past experience? Do you blame your past for your current financial situation? Do you believe this past experience is the reason, or one of the reasons why you struggle with relationships? Where do you find yourself blaming your past for your current circumstances? Do you ever say things like, *"If my parents/teachers/others didn't _____"* or *"If only my parents/teachers/others _____, I would be able to _____"?* Be honest about this. No one will see this except you, unless you choose to share it. The more honest you can be, the more you can free yourself from what is holding you back.

Before going to the next step, it is important for you to know that your interpretation of this event and what you made it mean about you and about others is only that—an interpretation. It isn't facts. The facts are the specifics about the event: your age, where it took place, the specific feelings you had about the situation itself *(fear, anger, hurt)*, not the feelings or thoughts you had about yourself or others *(e.g. I must be ugly. My father is mean, etc.).* This is the part that you made up.

Even if someone told you to your face that you were stupid or ugly, this does not mean that this is who you are. Whatever labels or judgments you gave others who were involved in this event does not mean this is who they are. No matter what happened in the past, we want you to know that everyone, including you, was doing the best they could with the tools they had. You do not know what was going on in the life or lives of others involved.

What if you could go back in time and change the impact of this event into something positive and empowering? Well, you can! You have something incredibly powerful called your mind and you can use your mind to recreate your memories and rewrite the *"script"* from your past so that you can be freed from the negative and limiting impact it's had in your life and move forward from a place of peace and joy.

Step 4: Rewriting the "Script"

Every experience you had was, or is, an opportunity for you to grow. Take another look at the experience you are exploring right now. If you feel that someone did something to you that caused you pain and suffering, are you willing to look at this person in a different way?

If so, begin by asking yourself, *"What did this experience teach me?"* Look for a positive trait or outcome that resulted from this experience. For example, did this experience help you develop compassion, patience, determination, persistence? If you can only think of a negative effect, ask yourself, *"If I were willing to look at this experience with a different perspective, what could I learn from it?"*

Now, imagine that the person or people involved were acting from a place of loving you so much that they did whatever they felt they had to do to protect you from getting hurt or from making a mistake that could possibly ruin your life. Or perhaps they were behaving from a place of being stressed and anxious about their own life and projected this onto you.

You have already taken the first 4 steps and now for the most powerful step of all...

Step 5: Forgiveness

Close your eyes and imagine this person, or all the people involved are sitting across from you right now. Imagine them telling you how sorry they are for what they did. Imagine them telling you how much they love you and didn't mean to hurt you. Imagine them telling you whatever it is that you need to hear so you can let go of the pain that you've attached to this memory.

See yourself forgiving them and forgiving yourself for allowing this experience to hold you back and stop you from living from a place of full, authentic expression. Allow yourself to be immersed in this positive experience and FEEL the love all around you. Bathe in this feeling for as long as you wish.

MESSAGE #10

CELEBRATE YOUR ACCOMPLISHMENTS

Where are you going? What is your destination? What are you striving for? Do you even know? Or are you blindly walking forward, or backwards, bumping into whatever is in your way and stumbling toward an unknown destination? What is driving you? On what basis do you make your choices every day? Is it based on what you want to do or what you think you have to do or what you think you should do?

So many of you get started on a path, often one that you didn't consciously choose, only to find yourself going in circles and wondering why you never seem to get anywhere. For others, it may be a path that began as a conscious choice but is driven by unconscious, limiting beliefs that keep you stuck.

Do you even know what you want...what you really want? Or have you resigned to what you think you can have, or what you think is possible for you?

We are here to remind you, once again, that ANYTHING and EVERYTHING is possible in the field of infinite possibilities! In order for you to tap into this infinite field, you must first believe it is there and then believe that you can access it at will.

When was the last time you stopped and really looked at your life?

For so many, life becomes a routine. One day moves into the next and the next and the next and soon each day begins to look and feel the same. You go into automatic mode and, as many of you call it, get *"stuck in a rut."* When you realize you are stuck in a rut or when you begin to notice that your life seems to be on auto pilot, this is wonderful. Why? Because this is the time you can choose to shift, to move in a new direction, one that is filled with excitement and passion, one that is truly aligned to your soul's purpose.

Many have asked the question, *"Why am I here?"* although few have taken the time to really look within to find the answer to this question. Instead, they search for it outside of themselves and the more they do so, the further away they get from their Truth. Over time, many get lost in the outer world and forget that who they ARE lives in their inner world.

It is wonderful that you have chosen to stop and reflect and turn around to come back to your Self. Yes, the outer world will still pull you and tempt you to stay on her path and the more you turn within, the fewer grips this outer world will have on you. Once you begin to get a glimpse of what lays within you, you will want to learn more and more. At times, you may be confronted and not want to see what is there, and we can promise you this. If you are willing to look past this discomfort and trust this process, as you get closer and closer to your true Self, you will be very pleased with what you see and with who you are.

You have to get past the barrier of lies and misperceptions in order to uncover the Truth.

If you are willing to accept that whenever you see something that brings up pain and suffering, this is not YOU, but yet another barrier to uncovering you, then you can look at what is bringing up this pain and suffering and see it for what it is: a block to the Truth and nothing more. You can let go of whatever stories you've been carrying around all these years about what caused this pain and suffering and simply let it go. As you let go more and more of who you are not, you will begin to see more clearly who you are.

We can tell you over and over again how beautiful you are, how gifted you are, how important you are, how lovable you are and yet, until you SEE this for yourself, you will be inclined to not believe us. You will continue to produce evidence that proves to you something different. But we do not accept this evidence that you produce, for we know it is not the Truth. It is false evidence disguised as the Truth.

It is time to take off this disguise and expose the Truth. You can do this, one step at a time. You are, in fact, already doing this. If you have done all of the exercises up to this point, you are already beginning to see the Truth and we hope that you are celebrating how far you've come and honoring yourself for your willingness and dedication to continue on this path.

You know deep within you that there is much more to you than you may have thought over the years, and you are beginning to accept this more and more. Congratulate yourself on how far you've come. You have done an amazing job at living your life. You've made it this far and your future is filled with such promise and such joy and such peace. It is all within your grasp. All you have to do is reach inside and take hold of it.

All that you desire awaits you and has always been available to you.

Now you are beginning to see the path more clearly: the path that leads you home, the path that leads you back to YOU. We are so excited to assist you on this journey and please call on us at ANY time.

Today, take some time to record everything you've accomplished in your life, everything you feel good about in your life, everything that makes you feel joyful when you think about it. If, during this process you find yourself thinking about and reliving a painful memory, go back to the last exercise and move through each step to release whatever is still lingering. If you notice negative thoughts popping into your awareness, use the tool for Transforming Negative Self Talk presented in Message #3. If painful emotions emerge, you may choose to repeat the words presented in Message #6 to help you work through them: Repeat the words. *"I let go of this feeling of_____, and I give thanks that I am creating room for my real Self to emerge."*

There are many ways for you to uncover and release painful memories and limiting beliefs and patterns that keep you stuck and that stop you from manifesting what you truly desire. One way is not better than another. If you found that the past exercise did not work for you, that is not a problem. If you've learned another method that works better for you, use it.

Explore various methods and choose the one that resonates with you the most, the one that you feel speaks to you and supports you in letting go and moving forward. Make it a daily practice to work with whichever process you choose so that piece by piece you will release the thoughts and beliefs that block you and replace them with more affirming thoughts and with an inner knowing that you have the power within you to easily and effortlessly create whatever you want. Below is a simple and quick, 3-step method you may find helpful.

Steps for Releasing Negative and Limiting Thoughts

* Take a deep breath and release it.

* Take another deep breath and release it. Repeat this a few times until you can feel your body fully relax.

* Declare any or all of the following affirmations **with belief and conviction** any time you catch yourself thinking a negative and/or limiting thought:

"I am a powerful and magnificent manifestor."

"I have the power within me to tap into infinite intelligence and infinite possibilities."

"I release any and all thoughts and beliefs that do not serve me or the highest good of all. I let them go with love and ask that these thoughts and limiting beliefs be transmuted and transformed into love and Light and may this new energy be added to the universal energy of Light and love for all to access."

"I ask that all my limiting beliefs and negative patterns be replaced with love and Light and a deep knowing that I am a co-creator with all that Is and that I can have, be and do whatever I desire."

Remember to go back to recording happy memories and allow yourself to relive these positive and uplifting moments and feel the joy; feel the excitement; feel the love. For this is who you are: Joy, Peace, and Love.

MESSAGE #11

WHAT ARE YOU AFRAID OF?

How does it feel for you to begin to uncover the Truth about who you are? Does it scare you or does it excite you? Or perhaps a bit of both? Whatever you feel is okay. Do your best to simply allow your feelings to be and to not judge them.

As we've mentioned before however, if you have a thought or a feeling that brings you down or has you falling back into negative patterns or behaviors, do your best to notice what is happening and then make a different choice, one that will empower you and lift you up.

What happens when you forget who you are? You begin to live the life of an impostor, and after a while, you also begin to believe that you ARE this impostor. You begin to identify with the characteristics of this impostor and believe this is who you are.

There are many impostors walking around your earth, many of whom have no idea that they have lost themselves somewhere along the way.

As you begin to wake up to the realization that you are not who you think you are, and as you begin to peel away the layers of untruths to reveal the true you, you will also begin to see those around you who are still asleep to this Truth. As you begin to see more clearly what is inside of you, you will also begin to see more clearly what is all around you. You will begin to notice more and more and understand yourself and others better.

Fear is one of the biggest disguises on your planet. It stops you from moving forward. It stops you from living your life to the fullest.

It stops you from just about anything and everything. The most destructive part of fear is that it stops you from being you.

When you are in fear, you cannot hear the small quiet voice within you because fear will drown it out every time.

Fear will dictate your actions and control your life...if you let it. Once fear has a hold of you, it is difficult for you to let it go, since fear feeds on itself and the more you fear, the stronger the fear becomes. Fear of the unknown is what keeps many stuck, fear of rejection, fear of making a mistake, fear of being alone, fear of death.

What are your biggest fears? What are your smaller fears? Make a list of everything you are afraid of that is holding you back, even if you don't think it is holding you back. You may have come to justify your fears and to convince yourself that it is good to have some fears. Even if you believe this to be true, write down these fears anyway. Uncover every stone and look deep within.

Once you feel complete, go back and read each fear and ask yourself, *"How has this fear impacted my life? What has this fear stopped me from doing, being or having? How could my life be different if I did not have this fear?"*

If at the end of this, you are ready to let go of your fears and to allow the positive energy of love to take its place, repeat the words, *"I let go of all my fears that are stopping me from living my true, authentic life. I let go and surrender to the Truth. I am open and receptive to allowing the energy of love to replace every fear, bringing me closer and closer to my true essence. Thank you, thank you, thank you."*

MESSAGE #12

A TIME TO REFLECT

My beloved child, there is so much we wish to share with you. We are so delighted that you are continuing along this path, this path of self-discovery, this path of remembering. It is with a joyous heart that we connect with you today as in every other day. You may be wondering why it is that you are here, in this moment. You may be questioning your life and where it is going. Fear not, for you are exactly where you need to be in this moment of time. All is truly in Divine Order, as some of you say. There are no mistakes, no accidents.

> *Even when you think or feel that things are falling apart, they are not. They are simply dissolving to make room for something greater, something beyond your imagination.*

You cannot go where you want to go without preparing yourself for it. Whenever you begin to doubt yourself or doubt the process, remember this: you would not have found yourself here if you were not ready. You ARE an incredible being of Light, one who was courageous enough to be on planet earth during a time of great transformation. You are much more than you think you are and much more than others may think you are. You have greatness within you. It is time to release all that is in your way of allowing this greatness to shine. The world needs you now and it is time to step aside from your smaller self and give birth to your true Self.

Let go of the past and all the stories around it. The past is over and all that happened in the past was required in order for you to be able to serve in a way that brings forth all that is possible for you and others. It is time to let go of blame, shame and fear and make way for Light, peace and love for this is who you are and who others really are.

You have no idea what awaits you and we are so excited for you and for all who choose to walk this path, this path to enlightenment and Truth. As you begin to shed what isn't real, you will be left with Truth. The Truth is that EVERYTHING is possible in the world of infinite possibilities. The only limitations you have are those you place on yourself. You are limitless. You are eternal. You are all that is and all that has been. You are one with all and all is one with you. As you begin to wake up to this Truth, you will begin to see this more and more clearly. First, you must let go of all that keeps you stuck, all that keeps you small, all that keeps you from expanding and growing.

If you have been integrating all that you've read so far and have completed the exercises thoughtfully and contemplatively, then you are already well on your way. If, for some reason, you've skipped some of the exercises or feel you didn't really take the time to delve deeply into them, go back and complete them now. Even if you've completed each and every exercise, we encourage you to go back and review each exercise and your responses to each and ask yourself if you would answer the same today.

As you re-read the past exercises and your responses, journal about whatever comes up for you. What thoughts and feelings are you experiencing as you go back and review? Are you feeling some shame about still holding on to some negative thinking or limiting thoughts? Are you feeling happy to recognize you've let go of some things that were previously holding you back?

There are no right or wrong answers. What is important is that you record the Truth about what you are thinking and feeling. It is through this truthful and authentic reflection that you will free yourself from what is still holding you back. Recording what you think you should be thinking or feeling will not serve you. No one is judging you here and we encourage you to not judge yourself about where you were when you first started this process and where you are right now.

Even if you are in the exact same place, that is okay. It is never too late to begin again. Just start wherever you are in this moment and take the next step...whatever that is for you. Your next step might be to start back at the beginning of this book and move through it more slowly, more reflectively. Your next step might be to recognize and celebrate how far you've come since beginning this process. Or, you may choose to do both. One is not better than the other. We cannot stress this enough. What is important is that you are here now and for this we give thanks.

MESSAGE #13

WHAT DO YOU CHOOSE TO BELIEVE?

What do you know to be true? How do you know it is true? Have you ever given thought to how you came to believe what you believe? Where did you first hear it? From a parent, teacher, clergyman or the media? What stops you from questioning all that you believe? Is it fear of the unknown? What would happen if you stopped and took a look at all that you believe to be true and asked yourself, *"Why do I believe this?"* Yes, it may be confronting, especially if you discover that all your beliefs came from outside of you.

What you believe dictates the direction of your life and all your life experiences. It is through your beliefs that you make choices that determine how you experience your world. Whether you believe it or not, you have the power to choose what you want to believe and through this, recreate your reality.

Take a look at those around you. What do you think they believe? All you have to do is look at how they live their lives and you can determine their beliefs. Listen to their conversations and you will know more about what they believe. You will also see a pattern of how one's beliefs are directly manifested into experiences. If you want to change anything in your life, you must first begin by changing your beliefs around it. If, for example, you want to change your financial situation, it is important to uncover all your beliefs around finances. You must dig deep to uncover the beliefs that are hidden deep within you and that are not part of your consciousness in this moment. You may be surprised to find beliefs that you didn't even know were there and these are the beliefs that have been running your life. You will also find that you have accumulated these beliefs throughout your lifetime beginning in childhood. You did not question these beliefs and simply accepted them as true because others did the same.

You have been learning how you can take control of your destiny and determine the direction you wish to take. With choice comes responsibility and you must be ready to accept responsibility for your choices if you wish to have power over them. You can't have it both ways. You can't claim to have power over your destiny and then blame others or circumstances for your experiences. It doesn't work that way. You either take responsibility for everything or you don't. It's that simple.

Today is a new day, just as every other day, a day when you can begin again to create whatever you want. Yes, we know you've been taught you can't always get what you want and we are here to tell you that this is not true. What is true is that you have forgotten what it is you have to BE in order to get or have what you want. You read that correctly. It is not about what you have to do. Let us explain.

If you are like most people, you've been taught from a very early age that you can't have everything you want and, for the most part, you will have to work hard to get what you want. You heard this so many times that you accepted this as the Truth. But look around you. Are there not many people who work very hard and still don't get what they want? You might be one of them.

Look again. Are there not many people who don't work very hard at all and seem to have everything? You may think that this is not fair and yet fairness has nothing to do with it. It has everything to do with what you believe and what you think on both a conscious and unconscious level.

Your unconscious mind is extremely powerful and is, in fact, running your life.

Just because many thoughts and beliefs are held in your unconscious mind, this doesn't mean you are not capable of becoming aware of them. All you have to do is look at your life. Your life is a direct manifestation of your deepest and strongest beliefs and thoughts. This can be both scary and exciting depending on how you choose to look at it. It will be scary if you believe you have no power over your thoughts or beliefs and exciting if you choose to believe you can change your beliefs and direct your thoughts. Where your life goes from here will depend on which one of these you choose.

If you choose to believe that you have no power over your thoughts or beliefs, you will be at the mercy of others and of circumstances, and will live your life from a place of reacting to what shows up in your life. If you choose to believe that you have the power to change your beliefs and direct your thoughts, AND if you are willing to do the work to uncover your hidden beliefs and thoughts, then ANYTHING is possible for you.

What do you choose to believe? We invite you to make a choice right now because your life depends on it.

If you choose to believe that there really isn't anything you can do to change your life or your circumstances, then there isn't much we can help you with. If you want to believe that you have the power within you to change your thoughts and beliefs and therefore to change your life, but you are not sure how to proceed from here, do not worry or concern yourself about this. You do not need to know how to do this since we are here to guide you to your Truth. We can only guide you, however, if you are willing to accept that you have the power within you to create the life you truly desire. So, once again, what do you choose to believe? Are you ready to take charge of your life and to look deep within you to see what is there? If so, let's continue.

Many of you are afraid to look within yourselves for fear of discovering things that you don't like or for fear of digging up past wounds that may cause you more pain and suffering. We are not suggesting that you look within yourself so that you can relive the past. As we've said before, the past is the past and reliving it will not serve you in the present moment. When we speak of looking within, it is to see what is there NOW, in this present moment, for this is what is creating your present moment experience. Let's explore this further with an example from your own life.

Think of something that you are experiencing in your life now that you are not happy with. Perhaps you do not have the relationship you want. Maybe you don't have the amount of money you want, or the job you want. Choose one thing that, if you had a magic wand, you would change. If possible, write it down.

Here are some possible ways of recording your current thoughts. Choose the one that resonates with you or write it in your own way.

"If I had a magic wand, I would _____."

"I wish _____."

"If only _____ then _____."

Next, answer the following 3 questions:

1. How would my life be different today if I had *[whatever you wrote above]*? Write in as much detail as possible.

2. I believe the reason(s) I don't have *[whatever you wrote above]* is because _____. Once again, record EVERY thought and belief you have about why you don't have this in your life right now. Be as honest as possible. Unless you are willing to be truthful about this, you will not be able to change it.

3. I believe that in order for me to have *[whatever you wrote above]*, I would have to _____. Record EVERYTHING you believe you would have to do or what you believe would have to take place in order for you to have this in your life.

Most of what you recorded for numbers 2 and 3 are likely limiting beliefs and thoughts that are stopping you from manifesting what you want in your life. If, in number 3 you included that you would have to change your thoughts and beliefs, this would be true.

So, how do you go about changing limiting thoughts and beliefs? First, by doing what you just did so that you can increase your awareness. If you don't even know what thoughts and/or beliefs are limiting you, then how could you possibly change them?

We encourage you to explore other areas of your life where you are not experiencing what you want and to answer the 3 questions above for each of them. Do your best not to judge yourself or your responses, and acknowledge yourself for your willingness to become more aware. This is a very important and essential step to manifesting whatever you desire.

MESSAGE #14

THE POWER OF THOUGHT

Have you ever wondered what it would be like to be happy all the time? Do you believe this is even possible? Well, it is! You have the capacity within you to be happy no matter what is going on around you. Believe it or not, being happy is a choice, just as being sad or angry or frustrated is a choice. Each of these, and any other emotion you feel, begins with a thought, a thought that you accept as Truth, whether consciously or unconsciously.

Are you beginning to see how powerful your thoughts are and how important it is for you to become more aware of your thoughts if you want to experience the life you truly desire? What thoughts are popping up for you now? Are they empowering thoughts or are they thoughts that will keep you stuck?

Behind every emotion is a thought, or a series of thoughts, that keep this emotion alive. The longer you hold on to these thoughts, the longer you will feel whatever it is that you are feeling. If you want to change what you are feeling, you will first have to become aware of what you are thinking and then choose a different thought, one that will draw forth what it is you wish to feel.

Your emotions are also extremely powerful. It is through your emotions that you attract your life experiences. Emotions carry with them a certain frequency or vibration that sends a message out to the Universe and brings to you experiences that match this frequency. Low frequencies, or vibrations like anger, sadness or frustration, will attract situations or circumstances that will match these emotions. In the same way, higher frequencies or vibrations, like happiness, gratitude and love, will attract to you experiences that will match these emotions.

No matter what you are feeling today or what you are currently experiencing in your life, the good news is that you have the power within you to change your thoughts and, as a result, change your emotions, which will then attract to you the experiences you desire.

How can you begin? With your thoughts, of course. Write down the following statement:

"I have the power within me to attract whatever I desire into my life."

Now, repeat this statement *(which is a thought)* to yourself and write down every other thought that pops into your mind when you say it. You may have thoughts like, *"No I don't. I have no control over what happens to me."* Or *"I have no idea how to do this."* Or *"This sounds like it is going to take a very long time."* Perhaps you may think, *"Yay! I can hardly wait to learn how to access this power!"*

How do you feel when these thoughts pop into your mind? Do these thoughts make you feel discouraged? Fearful? Excited? Keep repeating the above statement and record every thought and feeling that you become conscious of. Remember, the first step is to become aware of your thoughts and feelings, and then you can choose to focus on the thoughts and feelings that will attract to you what you really want.

Once you feel complete, write down the above statement on a card or small piece of paper and carry it with you or display it someplace where you will see it from time to time throughout your day. Repeat this statement as often as possible and, even if you are having trouble believing it is true, use your ability to *"act"* and pretend that it is true. Make a conscious decision to play the role that it is true, including acting out the emotions that you would feel if you believed this statement was true.

Use your imagination to help you *"feel"* what it would be like if you had the power to attract whatever you want into your life. Feel the excitement and the possibilities. Take only a few seconds at a time to do this. If you take longer, your mind may jump back to your conditioned thoughts of *"It's not possible."* or *"I'm only fooling myself."* What is important here is that you begin to move in a new direction and be patient with yourself. You didn't get where you are today overnight and it will take time for you to take back control over your thoughts and learn how to harness the power of your mind. You CAN do this and we will continue to guide you one step at a time.

MESSAGE #15

YOU ARE NEVER ALONE

Beloved child of God, you are so precious it is hard for words to describe. You have no idea just how important you are. We are so excited that you are beginning to see the Truth about who you are, for it is in remembering who you are that you will be able to serve those around you from a place of Divine love and peace.

Life was never meant to be a burden, but a gift...An opportunity to express your Divine Self in ways that have never been expressed before. Somewhere along the way you, like so many others, lost your way and also began to lose your connection to Source. As time went on, you forgot more and more and, as each generation appeared, this connection to Source became more difficult to sustain.

We have been waiting for this time for a long time. Now that more and more of you are waking up, we can see this connection to Source becoming brighter and brighter for all of humanity. Yes, we know it may appear on the outside that your world is falling apart and, on some level, it is, and that is wonderful because now you can work together to rebuild your world into what you always wanted and knew it could be. You can rebuild from a place of love, peace and abundance.

You have no idea, or perhaps you are beginning to understand, that you have the power to create anything and everything you desire. There are absolutely NO limits.

We understand that this may be difficult to comprehend, especially since so many of you are suffering a great deal. All we ask at this time is for you to be open to the possibility that what we are saying is true and be willing to continue to seek the Truth for as Jesus said, *"The Truth will set you free."*

Be filled with the knowledge of who you are. Once you truly connect to this Truth there is nothing that will stop you from achieving that which you desire. NOTHING will get in your way for you will be crystal clear about the direction you wish to take. This does not mean there will be no obstacles on your path. What it means is that you will find a way to move through each obstacle with grace and ease. You will not see the obstacle as a block but as an opportunity to use your gifts and talents to move through them. Fear will no longer have a hold on you and will not slow you down.

Be gentle with yourself as you move through this process for it has taken years for you to forget who you are and it will take time for you to sift through all the debris to find the gem that has been hidden.

Do not worry about how long it will take. Let go of feeling you are not doing it right or you *"should"* be further ahead by now. There is no limit to how much time you have. You have whatever time you need. We can only tell you that once you reconnect to the Truth of who you are, you will be amazed at what you will find and you will rejoice.

Your self-doubt and feelings of lack will diminish and you will be fully in your power. You may think this is impossible and we are here to tell you it is not only possible, it WILL happen for you, as long as you do not give up. Do not give up on yourself. Stay true to this process and do your best to let go, moment by moment, of each negative and limiting belief that pops into your mind. As you let go of these thoughts, you will find that over time they will be replaced with thoughts of certainty and you will feel more and more empowered. You will begin to find it easier and easier to let go of thoughts that do not serve you for you will begin to recognize them more quickly, before they take hold of you and bring you down.

If you have been following the steps with each message so far, and if you have been completing the exercises that have been suggested to support you in uncovering and remembering the Truth about who you are, then you are well on your way. Congratulate yourself for how far you've come. Rediscovering who you are is not an easy feat. It takes courage, persistence and determination to walk this path. It is much easier to follow the crowd, even if you suffer in the process, than it is to stand out among them and be SEEN for there are many among you who will try to bring you back down.

Your standing tall will confront those who are not ready to take this stand for themselves and the only way they can reduce their fear of taking a stand is to try to knock you down. Do your best not to judge these people for they are suffering a great deal and are very lost. What they need is your love and compassion and understanding. Also make sure to give this to yourself, for you need it too.

Seek to be among others like you who are also taking a stand for Truth and for rediscovering their true essence. There are many of you and the numbers are growing by the minute. Do your best to surround yourself with others who are on a similar path for you can encourage one another and help one another. When one of you is feeling discouraged, others can help you see the Truth and you can do the same for them.

You do not need to walk this path alone and, in fact, you are never alone.

We are with you always. We understand that you also feel the need to have other humans around you to support you and this is available to you as well. Open your eyes and we will show you where these people are so that you can connect with them and you can help one another. Together you will do many things and, as you strengthen yourself, you strengthen others.

Today, take stock of who is around you and who will support you on this path that you have chosen and who is also on a path of self-enlightenment. If you do not have anyone in physical form who understands this path you are on, do not fret. Take time to explore what is available in your community for those on a conscious, spiritual path. Look for a spiritual community that you can participate in. If you can't find a group, start one. If you have access to Internet, search for online groups or forums that have members seeking the Truth.

Even if you find only one other person, this is enough, for the two of you can help one another and you will see that, as your energy expands, you will attract others like you and you will connect with more and more people who are on a similar journey. Stay true to your path and to your Self and you will continue to attract others of like mind toward you. If you have no one right now, continue to connect to us daily and speak to us and share your hopes dreams and sorrows with us, for we are here for you and always will be.

MESSAGE #16

GOING DEEPER

Where do you begin when you want to create something for yourself? Do you make a wish and hope that it comes true? Do you tell yourself you are asking for too much? Do you wonder if you will ever have what you want? Do you believe that things happen by chance and that some people are just luckier than others? What is it that you believe when it comes to creating the life you truly desire?

What will it take for us to convince you that you have the power within you to create ANYTHING and EVERYTHING you want and nothing is too big or too small for you to manifest?

This is not to say that you can control others or determine what others do. We are speaking of YOU and YOUR life. If, for example, you wish to be in a loving relationship with another, it is important for you to be very clear on the essence of the type of relationship you want and the characteristics of the type of person you want. If you choose to focus on attracting a specific person into your life, you limit your possibilities and interfere with what is possible, for you do not know the entirety of the person on whom you are focusing and he/she may not be what you really want, but only what you think you want.

This is why it is so important to be clear on what it is you really want and to dig deeper into the core of why you want what you think you want. The deeper you go, the more likely you will manifest what you desire, and the more likely you will be happy with what you manifest. As you dig deeper, you may discover that what you really want is something very different from what appeared on the surface. Once you know what you want, it is important to believe that you can have it, for if you believe you are not capable of having it, or feel you are not worthy of it, then you are sending a message to the Universe that stops it from coming to you.

You are constantly sending messages to the Universe through your thoughts and energetic vibrations, whether you are aware of this or not.

If you are unsure about what thoughts or vibrations you are sending out, just take a look at where your life stands in this moment, since your current life is a direct reflection of the signals you have been sending out throughout your life. When it comes to Universal Laws, it does not matter what you believe for they are not dependent on beliefs and are at play at all times throughout the Universe. Much has been written in particular about the Law of Attraction and yet so few fully understand it. If you truly wish to experience a full and abundant life in all areas, it is worth taking time to learn more about this powerful Law so that you can use it to manifest your ideal life.

For today choose another area of your life that displeases you and that you wish to change. Perhaps you want more money, a better job, a loving relationship. Once you choose what you wish to focus on, complete this statement:

"I want _____ because if I had _____ I would _____."

Describe in detail how you feel your life would be different than it is today if you had this one thing that you really want.

Next, complete the following statement and take time to dig as deep as you can so you can uncover your limiting beliefs and thoughts that may be hidden:

"The reasons I don't already have _____ are because..."

    * Reason #1: _____.

    * Reason #2: _____.

List every reason or belief you have about why you don't have the relationship you want or the money you want or the job you want or whatever it is you want. If you wish, you may repeat this exercise focusing on other things that displease you and that you wish to manifest.

In order for you to manifest what you want, it is essential that you be willing to take 100% responsibility for your life. If you are not willing to do this and you choose instead to blame others or circumstances for your current life situation, then you are giving your power away and will continue to be a victim of circumstances and there is nothing we can do to help you. Once you take 100% responsibility for your life and ALL your creations, you open the door to unlimited possibilities! You have been given free will, so the choice is yours.

We invite you to make your choice right now. There is no wrong or right choice. Each choice will lead to a different result. So, what do you choose? If you choose NOT to take 100% responsibility for your life, then there is no point in continuing to read this book for it cannot help you and we bless you on your path. If you are ready to take 100% responsibility for your life, we invite you to make the following declaration and if possible, speak it aloud. Speak only that which you are ready and willing to own in this moment. If there are parts of the declaration that do not resonate with you at this time, then simply leave them out. Remember, you have free Will and everything is your choice.

Declaration:

"I [full name] willingly accept that I AM 100% responsible for my life and declare that I am the master of my creations. I invite only beings of the Highest Light to assist me in manifesting my desires and I give thanks for all my creations. I ask that all my creations be manifested in a way that is in the highest good of all."

We recommend that you speak this declaration aloud every morning before you start your day. Speak it with emotion and authority for this will send a stronger signal to the Universe that will better support you in your manifestations.

MESSAGE #17

THE IMPORTANCE OF SELF-LOVE

D o you wish to accomplish great things? What is stopping you? If only you knew, really knew, what awaits you on the other side of fear, on the other side of doubt, on the other side of despair. You are so close and yet so far from what you desire, and the only thing in the way is you, for you have the power and always did. It is time to reclaim this power and use it to not only serve yourself but the world.

***As we have said before, the world
needs you now more than ever.***

If you feel or believe that reclaiming your power is boastful or wrong, you have been misguided for it is in owning your power that you can empower others to do the same. Imagine what your world would be like if every being knew the Truth about who they are and owned their magnificence? There would be no war, no hunger, no violence among you for each of you would see the magnificence in the other and would encourage one another to be greater and to express your magnificence.

***It is not too late for you, or anyone else still
walking the earth, to rise up and be the
REAL YOU, not the "you" who you THINK
you are, but the YOU who you ARE!***

For many, this is a scary place to be because you have become comfortable in playing small, in confusion, in struggle. We are here to remind you that this is not your natural state. Your natural state and way of being is love, joy, and ease. We remind you again that you really can have, be and do anything you desire so long as you come from love. Love for yourself and for all of creation.

Do you love yourself?

If you hesitated even for a moment in saying, *"YES,"* then there is still work to be done. If you do not love yourself completely, are you WILLING to love yourself even if you find it difficult and if you are unsure how to get from where you are to a place of loving yourself fully? As long as you are WILLING, you WILL be guided to a place of self-love.

There is nothing you need to change about yourself before you can love yourself. We are speaking of unconditional love in its truest sense. We are talking about loving YOU and this has nothing to do with your personality, your body, your job, or anything outside of you. Many of you have difficulty loving yourself because you feel unworthy of love.

You came into this world as a Being of love, knowing the Truth about who you are, and over the years this eternal Being of pure love and infinite possibilities has forgotten this Truth and accepted the lies that have been passed down through the generations, the lies that have held you back for so long and caused you much grief and pain. You have the power within you to reclaim the Truth and to emerge from this darkness into pure love and Light.

It is important that you do your best not to go into overwhelm as you move through this process of rediscovering who you are. It can be both exciting and scary at the same time. You begin to see what is possible and you also see what you must let go of in order to create what you really want. This can sometimes be a painful process and we assure you, it will be well worth it.

On the other side of pain is freedom and joy and abundance and ALL that you desire to experience.

It fills us with such joy to be here and to witness your transformation. We know the journey you have been on has been difficult at times and we are delighted to assist you on your journey home...on your journey back to YOU. You are surrounded by love at all times even when you think you are alone. If you could see what we see at the core of your being, you would have no difficulty in loving yourself, for you would know the Truth about who you are...a Magnificent Being of Light and Pure Love.

Loving yourself is so important if you wish to live a full and abundant life. If you do not love yourself, you send out a signal to the Universe that you are not worthy of receiving what you desire. Take some time today to be with yourself in a nurturing way. Take yourself for a walk, have a relaxing bath, go for a massage. Do whatever feels nurturing for you. Treat yourself with love, kindness and compassion and whenever you notice you are beating yourself up or being unkind toward yourself with your thoughts or actions, remind yourself that you are a magnificent being of Light and you are here to be an example to others of what is possible and help lead them home. If you have difficulty believing this to be true, go back to what we've suggested before and act as if it is true and allow yourself to imagine what it would be like if this was true and immerse yourself in the feelings of what it would be like to know and live and breathe this Truth.

Continue to take one step at a time and trust that all is well. You may find it helpful to go back and redo some of the previous exercises. You may be surprised to see that you are not in the same place as when you began this journey.

MESSAGE #18

WHOSE VOICE ARE YOU LISTENING TO?

Today, let us begin by congratulating you for how far you've come and for your commitment to continue on this journey of self-discovery. You have been working on uncovering the Truth about who you are and reclaiming your power so that you can manifest anything and everything you desire. Let us continue on this path of self-love for this is an area that is so difficult for many. As we have said, loving yourself is important and without self-love you cannot create the life you desire for you will sabotage opportunities that are presented to you. This is most often unconscious and this is why you experience struggle and frustration and wonder what you are doing wrong.

You wonder why, after putting so much effort into something, that things don't turn out the way you want. The reason is very simple: on some level, you do not believe you deserve to have it or you do not believe you are capable of achieving it.

Belief is very important when it comes to manifesting. Trusting and surrendering are also required, and the first step is self-love.

Rejoice for you are coming home. No, we do not mean you are leaving your earthly body. We mean you are coming home to yourself. As you uncover the real you who has been buried for so long, you will begin to open up the doors to what is possible for you. As you begin to uncover your limiting beliefs, you will be able to access the power of infinite possibilities. As you uncover and connect to infinite possibilities, you will gain clarity around not only who you are, but why you are here. Perhaps you are already beginning to catch a glimpse of this and if not, do not worry, for your time will come.

Let us begin to explore this a little further. Why do you think you are here? Do you have a sense of it or does your mind go blank when you ask yourself this question? Remember when you used to know that anything was possible? Do you remember how it felt? Chances are you have forgotten and this is why you are here now with an open heart and a hungry soul wanting to reclaim this part of you. You are only a moment away from connecting to the real you.

> ### *The real you is but a breath away, waiting patiently for you to recognize her and to call her back and give her a voice.*

You see, every time you are happy, excited, grateful, or hopeful with a sense of positive expectancy, your true self is present, so you haven't really lost her at all. You've only not recognized her at times among the other voices that you also carry within you, the voices of past hurts and disappointments and the voices of others who judge you, making you think and believe that you are not enough.

We urge you to start paying more attention to whose voice you are listening to in any given moment. The more aware you are of this, the more power you will have to choose the voice of Truth. You may be wondering how to discern among all the voices in your head which one is coming from your Higher Self and believe it or not; this is very simple. It is the voice of love, the voice of encouragement, the voice of celebration, the voice of gratitude, the voice of possibility.

Any time you hear a voice telling you that you can't do it or you are not worthy or you are not smart enough or not capable...Any time you hear the voice of fear, doubt, anger, resentment, jealousy...These are not coming from your true self and these are not your voices at all. These are voices that you have adopted as your own and as Truth as a way of protecting yourself. Do not beat yourself up for this for it is a part of the human experience.

It is time to embrace all of these voices and to thank them and express appreciation to them for all they have done to serve you. Let each voice be heard, acknowledged and loved. Extending love to these voices does not mean you have to follow what they say. It simply means that by acknowledging them and thanking them, you can then choose to listen to the voice of Truth, the voice of empowerment, the voice that expresses your magnificence. Whenever you find yourself in a situation that displeases you or that confronts you, ask yourself which voice are you listening to in that moment. Once you become aware of this, you can then choose to listen to the voice that expresses your true essence, the voice that affirms you and believes in you, the voice that is kind, compassionate and loving.

As you begin to do this work, you may find that you experience more upsets and more frustration. Do not let this frighten you. Embrace these situations and turn them into opportunities to practice discernment. When you recognize which voice is in control, you can then decide if this is the voice you wish to be in control of the situation or not and, if not, simply thank this voice for speaking and then choose a more empowered voice.

It might help you to identify which voice is in control. Is it you as a younger child? Is it your mother or father or a teacher from the past? You will find as you pay closer attention to these voices that most often it is the voice of your younger self, your parents or guardians or others who had a significant influence in your formative years. Because these voices have been in control for most of your life, they are much louder than the voice of your true Self, your Higher Self. Pushing these voices away will not stop them from coming back. Being aware of the voices and knowing they are not your authentic voice does not mean they will no longer show up in your life. It is not about trying to turn these voices off or ignoring them, for this will simply make them louder for they are determined to be heard. It is about listening to what they are here to teach you about where you are along your path.

When you embrace each voice and look for the lesson in the voice, then you can thank each voice for helping you become more aware of the Truth.

These voices are not going to go away. However, as you acknowledge them and then begin to take your power back, your authentic voice will take a stronger stand and will be much more audible to you as the other voices take a back seat.

Today, take some time to look back at some of your response to previous exercises. See if you can identify whose voice was expressing itself in your responses and record their names next to each response. You may want to re-write the responses with names next to them. Look to see whose voice has been given the most power in your life. It could be the voice of your father, your mother or your younger self. Thank each of these voices for all they have done to protect you and let them know that you are now ready to take control of your life and they can sit back and enjoy the ride. Then take some time to celebrate YOU, the authentic YOU, the magnificent YOU.

MESSAGE #19

ACKNOWLEDGE EACH STEP

T oday is a new day, just as every other, a day when you can begin again no matter what has happened before, a day when you can choose again what you wish to be, do or have. What do you choose? Do you choose to recreate the past or do you choose to create something new?

Stay alert to the signs around you, the signs that are there to help guide you. They are everywhere but you often do not see them. You are too busy going about your day, often in a robotic fashion, to even notice them. You ask for what you want and wonder why you do not get it. It is because your asking is fleeting and your thoughts and actions do not match what you are asking for. There is a disconnect between what you want and what you think and how you act. You must be in alignment with all of these if you truly wish to manifest what you want. If one of these is *"off,"* or moving in a different direction, you are delaying the receiving of what you want.

We have been working with you with these concepts for a while now. Are you beginning to notice when your desires and your thoughts and actions do not match? If not, pay closer attention to these. When you see that your thoughts and actions do not match what you want, this awareness gives you an opportunity to make a different choice and to change your thoughts and/or your actions to better match your desires. This takes practice for you have been living most of your life on what some call *"auto pilot,"* in a robotic nature, not conscious of how you are being or what you are thinking.

If you do not consciously begin to pay attention to your thoughts and actions, you will continue to experience the same things over and over again. Only you can put a stop to this. Only you can change the direction of your life and begin to walk a different path. There are always many paths before you and you are the one who chooses which one to take. You are the one who can choose at any time to change paths and walk in a new direction, one that is aligned with what you truly desire. If you do not believe you have this power, then you cannot access it and put it to work for you. Instead, you give your power away and will feel powerless because, in fact, in these circumstances you are powerless, but only because you choose to be.

Do not beat yourself up for anything, for this too is a choice. Instead, choose to celebrate your new awareness, your new insights. Be thankful for this and fill your heart with joy for having this awareness, and then use it to support you in moving toward your desires.

You are capable of creating and manifesting anything your heart desires, but only if you are willing to accept the Truth about who you are. When you KNOW this Truth and tap into your magnificence, there are no limits.

You may be thinking, *"Well what about people who desire to control others and manipulate them and have power over them? If anyone can have what they desire is this also not a possibility?"* The Truth is that no one can have power over another or manipulate them without consent and this consent is often unconscious. If everyone was connected to their true essence, they would not give their power away and, in fact, if everyone was connected to the Truth of who they really are, no one would have the desire to take away someone else's power for they would know this is not necessary in order to have what they want.

There are many in your world who strive to control others and to control conditions and who want power over them. This is because they do not realize they have the power within themselves. This is because they come from a place of lack and believe they must take from others in order to have for themselves. This is another lie that has been passed down from generation to generation. It simply isn't true.

There is more than enough of everything for everyone to flourish and when more and more people tap into their inner power they will also tap into Universal and Source energy, which is infinite.

There are no limits to what is possible in the world of creation. If everyone believed this to be true, there would be no fear of running out of anything, including clean water or clean air or energy to fuel your other creations, for you and others would simply create something new that would provide you with everything you want.

Are you beginning to see what we are trying to show you? The possibilities are massive and expansive and never ending. It is important to focus on yourself and to remember who you are so that you can join with the others who have done so and together create a larger field of energy making it easier for others to follow you. You are here now, tapping into this energy field that others are holding for you, both earthly beings and non-physical beings and, as you begin to shine your Light brighter, this field will expand and more and more will join us. Your Light matters. YOU matter.

We need you and your Light to assist us in co-creating a world of peace, joy and abundance for all.

We thank you for your interest and for your desire to walk this path of self-discovery and self-empowerment and we acknowledge you for how far you've come. We know the path you've been on has not been an easy one and we hope you are beginning to feel your load lighten. Continue to walk along this path, one step at a time, and do not fret when you stumble or fall. Reach out and take our hand for we are here to help you get up and continue along your way. You CAN do this. In fact, you ARE doing it right now. Look how far you've come. Thank yourself for your willingness to continue to walk along this path even when faced with doubt and uncertainty. Thank yourself for being here now.

Look for opportunities throughout the day when you can acknowledge yourself. Perhaps you will notice when you are having a thought that does not support you. As soon as you notice this, acknowledge yourself and tell yourself how wonderful it is that you noticed this. Then choose another more empowering thought. If you notice yourself appreciating someone or something, acknowledge yourself for choosing appreciation in that moment. Nothing is too small for you to take a moment to acknowledge yourself. As you acknowledge yourself more and more, rather than waiting for others to do this for you, you will feel more and more empowered and will see more and more the Truth about who you really are.

MESSAGE #20

BE AUTHENTIC

Happiness is a choice. There will be many who will disagree with this statement and this too is a choice. Until you are ready to accept the Truth about this, you will never experience the freedom of true happiness. Choosing to be happy does not mean you will never experience moments of sadness or grief. Choosing to be happy does not mean you must deny other feelings. What it means is that you acknowledge whatever you are feeling in the moment and then let it go, rather than holding on to it and allowing it to consume you.

Are you happy? If not, why not? Are you holding on to thoughts or to situations that do not serve you? Are you afraid of making changes in your life that can lead you to a more fulfilled and happy existence? What are you afraid of? If you were not afraid, what changes would you make in your life right now?

Until you are ready to face your fears and move through them, they will have control over you and will keep you stuck.

Fear is a state of being and you must decide if you will allow your fear to rule your life or not. Everyone experiences fear from time to time and those who are willing to move through their fears get to the other side where everything they desire is waiting for them.

Why are you so afraid to speak your Truth, to BE your Truth? You live in a world that is filled with promise for a brighter future, and the only way to live into this future is to be authentically YOU. Not the *"you"* that you have been conditioned to be, but the real you. It is the real you who will save this planet and save humanity. We invite the real you to please stand up. Stand up and face the Truth. Stand up and speak the Truth. Stop hiding behind the lies of comfort, the lies of mediocrity, the lies of what you perceive to be safety. Whenever you choose to hold back your Truth and to not show up authentically in the world, you add to the darkness and the despair.

We do not say this to fill you with guilt, but to awaken you and to let you know that holding back your Truth under the guise of protecting others from suffering is not protecting them at all and is causing you all to suffer. It takes great courage to speak your Truth when you know you will, or might, be judged by those around you. Stand in your magnificence and, when you do, you will no longer be concerned about the judgment of others for you will know that their judgment comes from their own feelings of lack and of self-judgment and are not about you at all. Remember, what others think about you and what others believe about you is not YOU. It is simply their perception of you that is, or has been constructed, based on false and limiting beliefs and based on the filters that have clouded their judgment for some time.

It is time for you to step out from the crowd and take your place among others who are doing the same.

As you step out in courage, you will be strengthened by those who have stepped out in front of you and you will then be able to help lead those who are following behind. It is like a chain that gets stronger as each link is added to it. You can do this even if that loud voice within you is saying you can't or it's too risky. Remember, the loud voice of fear is not trying to protect you, but to hold you back, for once you break through your fears and stand in your power, you will be unstoppable and you will see so clearly all the illusions you previously accepted as Truth. You will also see the illusions that others are still trapped in and can reach out and help those who are ready to also break free. It all begins with you.

Your life is about you and how you choose to show up in this world. Yes, you have faced all kinds of circumstances in your life, some that have been pleasant and some challenging. How you responded or reacted to each of these past events was based on a choice, whether this choice was conscious or not. Now that you are becoming more aware of the Truth, you can make more conscious choices that will lead you to the experiences you would like to have. Keep in mind that this will take practice since, if you are like most people, you have been living your life unconsciously most of the time, blaming others or circumstances for your lot in life.

Take comfort in knowing you are not alone on this path and as you begin to walk the path of authenticity, you will meet others who are on the same path and you can support and encourage one another along the way. As you walk this path, you will find it to be both scary and exciting at the same time. At times, your fear might be stronger and this is okay. Continue to take one step at a time and get the support of a friend, a coach or a mentor who can hold your hand and help you get up when you fall. As we've said before, you do not need to do this alone. There is no honor in doing so. If you have thoughts that tell you that you don't need any help and you can do it yourself, simply recognize that this is the voice of your Ego mind and make the choice to listen to your Higher mind and reach out to others.

Take some time today to reflect on areas in your life where you are not showing up authentically. With whom do you tend to hold back your Truth? Is it with a spouse, a co-worker, a friend? What stops you from being completely truthful with these people or in these circumstances? The more honest you are willing to be with yourself, the easier it will be to break free and to live an authentic and fulfilling life.

If you can take the time to journal about this, you will find yourself able to go deeper and deeper into what stops you from speaking authentically in the world. Remember, this is not about judging yourself or beating yourself up. It is about increasing your awareness and raising your level of consciousness so that you can create and live the life you truly desire rather than settle for whatever shows up.

MESSAGE #21

RELEASING LIMITING THOUGHTS & BELIEFS

Take a moment to reflect. Where are you going? Do you even know? Or are you blindly walking forward bumping into whatever is in your way and stumbling toward a destination unknown? So many of you get started on a path, often one that you didn't consciously choose only to find yourself going in circles and wondering why you never seem to get anywhere. For others, it may be a path of choice and yet you still find yourself getting lost along the way to what you think you want. Do you even know what you want, what you really want? Or, have you resigned to what you think you can have or what you think is possible for you?

We are here to remind you, once again, that ANYTHING and EVERYTHING is possible in the field of infinite possibilities!

In order for you to tap into this infinite field, you must first believe it is there and then believe that you can access it at will. There are many ways for you to uncover and release limiting beliefs and patterns that keep you stuck and which stop you from manifesting what you truly desire. One way is not better than another. Explore the various ways that have been made available to you and choose the one that resonates with you the most, the one that you feel speaks to you. Make it a daily practice to work with whichever process you choose, so that piece by piece you will release the limiting thoughts and beliefs that block you and replace them with more affirming thoughts and with an inner knowing that you have the power within you to create whatever you want and to attract it to you easily and effortlessly.

Here is another method you may wish to experiment with whenever you become aware of a limiting thought or belief.

*Take a deep breath and release it fully. Take another deep breath and release it. Repeat this a few times until you can feel your body relax.

*Repeat the following statements with feeling and expression (out loud if possible).

I am a powerful and magnificent manifestor.

I have the power within me to tap into infinite intelligence and infinite possibilities.

I release any and all thoughts and beliefs that do not serve me or the highest good of all. I let them go with love and ask that these thoughts and limiting beliefs be transmuted and transformed into love and Light and may this new energy be added to the universal energy of Light and love for all to access.

I ask that all my limiting beliefs and negative patterns be replaced with love and Light and a deep knowing that I am a co-creator with all that Is and that I can have, be and do whatever I desire.

*Take a few more deep breaths and feel the energy of the words within and around you.

MESSAGE #22

PUT AN END TO STRUGGLE

My dearest child, why do you continue to choose to struggle when all that you desire is within your reach? You have access to all that you desire within you. You simply have to claim it and it is yours. It really is that easy but, instead of owning what is yours, you seem to have a need to strive for it, to work for it, to struggle for it. This is not necessary.

If only you knew how truly magnificent you are! You would laugh at the silliness of it all. You would let go, once and for all, of all your doubts, fears and illusions and live in Truth. In Truth, you would manifest everything you desire easily and effortlessly for you would know, without doubt, that you are not only capable of this, but you were born for this.

> *Your life is an extension of Source itself who*
> *lives and breathes and expands through*
> *you and the experiences you choose.*

Source does not judge experiences as good or bad, right or wrong. They are simply experiences. If you do not like or enjoy what you are experiencing, then you do not have to continue with it for you have free Will and the power to choose whatever experiences you want. You must be willing, however, to let go of whatever is keeping you stuck in what you do not want, for you cannot hold on to what you do not want and manifest what you do want at the same time. You have been moving through a number of processes of uncovering your blocks, fears and illusions and by now you are beginning to catch a glimpse of what is possible for you. In Truth, ANYTHING is possible for you, but only if you believe this to be true, for your possibilities are limited only by your own mind and your own imagination.

Remember what we shared before: as you walk this path of remembering who you are, you will meet others along the way, some who are seeking Truth as you are and others who are so stuck in their fear and in their illusions that they will be confronted by your very presence. You see, as you begin to shed the layers of self-doubt and self-condemnation, your true essence will begin to shine and you will be emitting a Light that will draw to you others who are seeking Truth. At the same time, those who are confronted by your Light will attempt to cause you to turn out your Light and draw you back into darkness. They will do this by creating circumstances that will cause you to experience doubt and/or confusion and, if you allow these feelings to overpower you, your Light will be dimmed or extinguished.

You may have people very close to you, family and friends, who are not ready to face the Truth and who may try to bring you back to their version of reality. As they see you begin to expand and grow, they will be faced with a reflection of their own illusions and will either be inspired and join you or feel confronted and do everything they can to stop you. Continue to do your best not to judge them for they are acting out of fear. Also do your best to hold on to your Truth in the face of opposition.

It is extremely important for you at this time to surround yourself with others who are on a path of enlightenment so that you can support one another and keep one another strong when faced with resistance from others. You can help one another remember the Truth about who you are when you are not strong enough to hold on to this Truth on your own.

If you haven't already done so, take time today to look for empowerment groups within your community or online where you can become a member. If you can't find what you are looking for, start your own group. There are many like you who are seeking Truth and who need the support of a loving, caring and supportive community. We repeat...You do not need to walk this path alone for this too is a choice. There is no glory in saying, *"I did it myself!"* The true glory is in BEING yourself and you will find it much easier to find and hold on to your Truth if you connect with at least one other person who shares this vision and is willing to support you along the way.

MESSAGE #23

SURRENDER & TRUST

H ere you are again, ready and waiting for your next step. This is wonderful. Each step you take is bringing you closer and closer to the Truth...to YOUR Truth to Your Self. This is a journey that never ends for as you discover more and more about who you are, you will understand that YOU have no end. You will continue to expand into more and more and will be able to manifest more and more.

You are unlimited and so too are the possibilities of your manifestations. Even though at some point, you will leave your earthly body, this does not mean your journey of life has come to an end. No, it will simply evolve into another expression of who you are. For now, it is best to focus on this part of your journey for it is the journey itself that will reveal to you the Truth.

Life is not about getting to any particular destination for once you reach whatever destination you think you want to experience, you will have the desire to reach a new destination.

This is why it is so important to enjoy the journey itself, for this is what makes up your life. For many of you, the destination becomes the focus and you miss out on all the wonderful experiences you can have along the way. You are not present to the moment to moment experiences, because all you can see is the striving to get somewhere and the disappointments and frustrations of not being there yet.

Can't you see, there is nowhere to go in order for you to experience joy and bliss? You can experience it right now and in every moment if you choose to. This does not mean there is no point in moving toward a desired outcome or a desired destination. What it means is to be present along the way and to take time to enjoy the journey itself and let go of the need to be there now, wherever "there" is.

Do you understand what we are saying? How much of your life have you felt unsatisfied, wishing you had more money or a better job or a better relationship? How long have you been telling yourself that your life would be so much better *"if only..."*? No matter what your life looks like today and no matter where you want it to go, you can choose to be grateful for all that *"is."* The more grateful you are for what *"is,"* the more easily you can manifest what you desire. We are not saying you should only be grateful for what you have and not want more. It is wonderful to want more and more for you are a co-creator with the capacity to manifest endlessly. What we are saying is that if you fill your energy field with thoughts and feelings of being unsatisfied, angry, disappointed, frustrated at not being, doing or having what you want, not only will it be difficult to manifest what you desire but you will experience struggle and challenge along the way.

Think about it this way. If you really enjoy celebrating specific occasions like birthdays, anniversaries, reunions, etc. do you get angry every time you think about these occasions and feel frustrated because the celebration is not happening today? Do you make yourself wrong because you have to wait for the celebration to occur? No, you look forward to this occasion and feel excited with anticipation for when the day arrives. Every time you think about this upcoming celebration, you are filled with joy and happiness. The reason for this is because you trust that the day will arrive. You don't tell yourself things like. *"I can't believe the birthday isn't here yet. What am I doing wrong? Maybe I need to work harder so I can manifest the birthday sooner."* Trusting and knowing that the day will arrive allows you to enjoy the days leading up to the celebration. It allows you to prepare for the day with positive and uplifting feelings.

We invite you to trust that ALL you desire
is on its way to you and will arrive
at the right and perfect time.

As you wait for the day to arrive, prepare for the day with excitement and anticipation knowing it is only a matter of time before you experience the manifestation of your desires. Stay in a positive energy field of knowing and trusting that whatever your heart desires is on its way. If you have trouble believing this, go back to pretending. Imagine how you would feel if you knew deep within you that what you desire most is on its way and the arrival date will be a surprise.

Today, think of one thing that you desire most. Is it a new or better relationship? A better job? More clients for your business? A new house? More money? Take a few moments to imagine what your life will be like when this desire becomes real for you. Put yourself there now in your mind's eye and feel the happiness, the excitement of living in this reality.

Give thanks knowing that you will receive whatever it is you are asking for, or better. Ask yourself, *"How can I prepare for what I'm asking for?"* Just like you would make preparations in advance for an upcoming birthday party, you can also make preparations for receiving what you ask for. This is what is meant by what others have said, *"Act as if what you want is already here."*

What would you do if you knew without doubt that whatever you asked for is on its way to you? If you find it helpful, write down the thoughts that come to you. For example, if you are asking for a better and more fulfilling job, perhaps you might begin telling your friends and acquaintances about the type of job you are looking for and ask them to let you know if they hear about anything. You might attend various networking events. What is important here is that you continue to take steps toward what you desire, knowing that you will have it. Let go of *"when"* it will happen for, if you focus on this, you will find yourself feeling discouraged and frustrated when *"it"* doesn't happen soon enough. You will begin to doubt that it will happen at all and possibly give up.

Do your best to surrender and trust that whatever you desire will come to you and when you find yourself feeling discouraged or doubtful, remind yourself that this is similar to choosing to celebrate a birthday. The only difference is that with the birthday, you know the exact date when the party will manifest whereas with many of your other desires, the arrival date is unknown. We assure you that the arrival date will come as long as you continue to trust and believe that it will come and continue to walk towards it.

Below is a simple and yet powerful prayer that you can repeat through the day to support you in staying focused on what you want and believing it is on its way.

> *Dear God/Universe/Higher Power [whatever name resonates with you],*
>
> *I give thanks for [what you want] that is on its way to me. I am so excited about this [job, relationship, etc.] and can hardly wait for it to arrive. Show me what steps I can take that will bring me closer to this manifestation of my heart's desire or to something better. I surrender and trust that all will unfold in the right and perfect way at the right and perfect time. And so it is!*

MESSAGE #24

YOUR TRUE LIFE PURPOSE

Take a moment and breathe. Breathe into this day, this moment. Give thanks for your breath and the ease with which your body breathes. Do you even have to think about this in order for it to happen? No, it is a natural and necessary process in order to keep your body alive. Just as it is natural for you to breathe, it is also your natural state to be happy and to manifest all that you desire.

The reason you do not experience manifestation with as much ease as taking in a breath is because your thinking has interfered with this process.

In order for you to return to your natural state of effortless manifestation, you must first release your limited thinking and, in order to do this, you must first become aware of your limiting thoughts. If you have been working through the various exercises presented so far, you have already begun this process and, if not, we invite you to go back and complete the exercises. As you begin to notice more and more the thoughts that block your manifestations, you will be guided toward the Truth and more of your unconscious limiting beliefs will be brought to the surface so you can release these as well.

You may have already learned that it is your unconscious, limiting beliefs that direct your life and determine the results of your manifestations and at first this can feel discouraging. You may wonder what you can do if you *"don't know what you don't know"* as some have put it. The simple act of being WILLING to uncover your unconscious, limiting beliefs will help bring them to the surface and into your awareness, giving you an opportunity to let them go and replace them with more empowering thoughts and beliefs that are based on Truth.

> ***One of the most limiting beliefs that many of you have adopted as Truth is that you were born with a very specific life purpose about what you are here to DO.***

You have been told that unless you discover and live out this purpose you will not be happy or feel fulfilled. This has created much stress and distress for many of you who now have a strong desire to KNOW your life purpose so you can DO what you believe you are here to do. You read books and seek help desperately trying to figure out what you are here to do and most of you are driven by the fear of possibly never figuring this out and ending up with a life with no meaning. Take a breath and let this go. There is no right or wrong thing for you to do in this life. Your true purpose has nothing at all to do with what you choose to DO. It is all about who you are BEING.

You see, everyone's life purpose is the same, to BE your true, authentic self so that your magnificence will shine forth extending love and Light to ALL. Just imagine what your world would be like and what the quality of life would be for you and others if everyone on your planet knew the Truth about who they really are and lived from this place of Truth! It would be and can be spectacular!

As you begin to KNOW yourself, you will be naturally drawn toward various activities and will take action based on love and not fear. You will feel a calling deep within your soul that will be as natural as your breath, guiding you step by step. It will not take effort to *"figure out"* what you *"should"* be doing. You will be led, easily and effortlessly, along a path that brings you and others joy. This is what is natural, not the striving to become who you think you are supposed to be, or the stress of trying to decide what you are supposed to be doing.

In Truth, you can DO anything you want and you can feel happy and fulfilled DOING anything as long as you are doing it from a place of BEING your authentic self.

Jesus said, *"know thyself"*, for he knew that this is the true path to experiencing heaven on earth. If you read about any of the great mystics and spiritual leaders, they all emphasize the importance of looking within and seeing who you truly are.

Today take some time to reflect on how this message *"speaks"* to you. What thoughts and feelings came up for you as you read the words? Do you feel relieved? Disappointed? Angry? Whatever you are feeling is wonderful. We encourage you to go deeper into the feelings to see what is underneath. What thoughts and/or beliefs do you have that are causing you to feel the way you do?

MESSAGE #25

EMBRACING YOUR EGO

What makes your soul sing? What makes you feel alive...fully alive? Whatever it is, give yourself permission to immerse yourself in whatever activities bring you joy for this is your life purpose...to live in joy and in full expression of WHO YOU ARE!!!

You may have noticed that we keep coming back to the same place. You keep looking for a different answer, thinking it must be more complex than that, and yet it isn't. What is complex is unraveling all the layers that have been hiding the Truth. As you uncover one layer, another will pop up. Do not let this discourage you. Celebrate each step you take along this path for it is bringing you closer and closer to your true essence. When you are able to see who you truly are, this does not mean you have arrived at your destination. It means you are ready to step into your magnificence and co-create from this place of Truth, from a place of unlimited possibilities.

You must stop expecting or needing others to validate you and begin to validate yourself. This is an *"inside job."* It does not matter what others think about you because what they think about you says more about them than you. Keep in mind that the desire for outside validation comes from your Ego who is the source of all your doubt, confusion and lack of self-love. When you notice your Ego expressing itself through you, give thanks for this is an opportunity for you to see more of what is limiting you and stopping you from experiencing the life you desire. Pay attention to what your Ego is saying so that you can become aware of your blocks and limiting beliefs. Remember, awareness is the first step to transformation. You must first be aware before you can make a conscious choice to move in a new and more empowering direction.

Your Ego is a great gift and, if you can love and accept your Ego, rather than express anger and resentment toward it and wish it would go away, it can serve you rather than have power over you.

When your Ego presents you with a limiting and disempowering thought like, _"You can't do that,"_ or _"You better not try that, you will fail,"_ or _"You are never going to find your soulmate,"_ you can use these thoughts as opportunities for growth. Rather than letting these types of thoughts stop you from moving forward or from believing in yourself and your ability to manifest all that you desire, take a moment to thank your Ego for revealing this block and remind yourself that ALL limiting beliefs are lies. Call on your Higher Self and ask for the assistance of your non-physical guides to make a decision in that moment to replace the negative thought with the Truth, whatever it may be. Take a few moments to anchor this Truth by not only saying words like, _"I CAN do this,"_ or _"I WILL succeed,"_ or _"I am happy and grateful now that my soulmate is on his/her way to me,"_ but also FEELING the Truth of these statements.

We cannot emphasize enough the importance of FEELING the Truth behind the empowering words you tell yourself.

Your Ego has very strong feelings about its beliefs and this is what has kept your Ego strong and in charge of your life. If you truly wish to put your Higher Self in the driver seat, you must understand that the emotions you express when replacing Ego thoughts with more empowering thoughts must be of greater intensity than the Ego thought. It is also important for you to understand that your Ego will fight to stay in charge and will do whatever it can to keep its hold on you. This is why you find it so difficult to break free from the Ego. When you begin to move toward your authentic Self and your Ego presents itself in a stronger way, you back down.

Your Ego has been running the show for a very long time and likes to be in charge. If your Ego feels threatened in any way, it will flex its muscles to frighten you into submission and let's face it, up until now, this has been working very well. Just like it can be challenging to break a habit, it can be equally, if not more challenging, to break free of your Ego. The best way to do this is to embrace your Ego rather than fight it. Fighting your Ego actually makes it stronger since negative energy and vibration feeds the Ego. Embracing and loving your Ego and seeing it as a gift, on the other hand, will soften its hold on you since it will still feel important and will no longer fear being rejected or abandoned.

Take a few moments to reflect on today's message and record any Ego thoughts that pop up for you. Remember, it is not about stopping these thoughts from emerging, it is about embracing them and allowing them to express themselves to you so that you can uncover the Truth beneath the words and embody them. Give thanks to your Ego for helping you expand your awareness.

MESSAGE #26

PRISON OR FREEDOM...
YOU HOLD THE KEY

D o you remember when you were a small child? What thoughts come up for you as you look back? Do these thoughts fill you with joy or sadness? Just as past thoughts conjure up emotions within you, so does every thought you think in every moment. Were you able to put your attention on your past? Of course you were, because you have the power to CHOOSE what to think about in every moment.

The problem is you do not use this power to choose and instead allow external circumstances to choose your thoughts for you. You go about your day with random thoughts floating around in your head causing you to feel all kinds of things, some pleasant and some not, depending on which thought you are unconsciously focusing upon. It takes discipline to pay attention to your thoughts so you can manage them and, unless you make a conscious choice to do so, you will be at the mercy of whichever thought takes hold of you in every moment. You become a prisoner of your thoughts.

The good news is that you hold the key to set yourself free. Are you ready to set yourself free and take responsibility for your life? That's right! This key does not just release you from being held hostage by your thoughts, it releases you from being held back or bound by every limitation or block you are currently experiencing in your life.

***The key is taking 100% responsibility for
your life. No more blaming others
or circumstances for anything.***

As soon as you stop taking responsibility for something, you are putting yourself back in prison, for in that moment, you are no longer free and have given up your power to something outside of yourself. Your power is within you and is available to you in every moment and in every situation. You, however, must call upon this power and must be willing to look within and see the Truth in every situation. This can be difficult at times, for it is much easier to point the finger and blame others or blame an external situation for what isn't working in your life. *"If only they did this or that,"* you say, *"my life would be so much better and I wouldn't be so upset."* Or *"If I had more money, I would be so much happier and less stressed."*

Whenever you catch yourself with imprisoning thoughts like these, just remember that you hold the key and can free yourself in any moment. As soon as you take back 100% responsibility, you are free to make new choices that will result in new experiences and new outcomes. This is a process and does not mean that as soon as you decide to take responsibility and change your thoughts that you will instantly manifest what you want in the next moment. You must be willing to continue to manage your thoughts and make conscious choices in every moment, even when it may appear that nothing is changing and that this isn't working. If you give up and go back to your old ways of thinking and being, you will continue to experience what you don't want.

> *You are where you are today because of the accumulation of your past thoughts and choices, whether made consciously or unconsciously, and your future will be based on the dominant thoughts you focus on today and every day forward.*

We cannot stress enough the importance of paying attention to your thoughts and making a conscious choice to shift your thoughts whenever you notice they are imprisoning you. At first, this will seem laborious and tedious and, just as any new skill, the more you practice it the more automatic it will become. If you truly desire to take back the power that is yours, the power to manifest anything and everything you desire, then you must also be willing to do the work, the inner work that is required for you to access this power. This is also a choice and now that you know this is what it will take, you can choose to stay in prison, where it might feel safer and more familiar to you, or you can choose to use your key and courageously step out of your prison cell and into the unknown where infinite possibilities exist. What do you choose?

If you choose to stay in prison, there isn't much we can do to help you except to remind you that you hold the key and can use it at any time. If you choose to free yourself, we are here to help you keep yourself free or to help you to free yourself every time you notice you put yourself back into your cell. As we already said, this is a process and even if you decide in this moment to free yourself, you will unconsciously put yourself back in prison from time to time since this has been your automatic way of being. Do not fret when you find yourself back in your cell, just notice you are there and powerfully take your key and let yourself out and continue along your freedom path. The more you do this, the stronger and more empowered you will become and at some point, walking along the freedom path will become automatic for you.

To assist you in becoming more mindful of where you are in a given moment, in prison or along the freedom path, we recommend that you create a way for you to *"check in"* with what you are thinking and feeling at various times throughout the day. You may want to set an alarm on your watch, computer or cell phone. We recommend you *"check in"* every hour when you first begin. When your alarm goes off, take a few moments, to notice what you are thinking and feeling. If you can take a moment to quickly jot down and record what you notice on paper or an online journal, that would be great and if not, that's okay. If you notice your thoughts and feelings are limiting and feeling unpleasant, use this as an opportunity to take out your *"key"* of responsibility and consciously shift your thoughts and freely walk away. If you notice your thoughts and feelings are empowering and positive, record this, if possible, and celebrate and acknowledge yourself for being on your freedom path.

As you begin to notice yourself being on your freedom path more and more, begin to *"check in"* every couple of hours and then every few hours until you notice you are spending most of your time on your freedom path. At this point we recommend you take a few moments at the end of each day to *"check in"* to see if there were any times throughout the day when you gave your power away and what you could do in future, similar situations to hold on to your power. It is equally, if not more important, for you to also celebrate and acknowledge yourself for all the moments when you took 100% responsibility for your actions and results. The more mindful you become of your thoughts and actions, the more easily you will be able to manifest what you want in life.

MESSAGE #27

STEPPING OUT
FROM THE CROWD

Stepping out from the crowd makes you more visible and this is what stops many of you from taking this step. You are afraid of being seen. You are afraid of becoming a target for others who may try to shoot you down, make you conform, or try to pull you back to where you once stood among them. Do not let this stop you, for it is the others who are afraid of you. When you step out, others are put in a position where they must either pull you back into the fold or look at what has been stopping them from taking this step. It is much easier for them to focus on you than on themselves.

We understand how frightening it can be when you step into the unknown, the unfamiliar, especially when you do not have those around you supporting you and cheering you on. We want to encourage you to stand tall and look within for the support you need for this you can always rely on. At first, it may not feel like enough for you are used to how things used to be and, even if it was painful, it was familiar and there is comfort in familiarity.

We are here to tell you that there is so much more
for you to experience in this life, more than
you can imagine in this moment.

If you are willing to look more deeply within, you will know that this is true. Hold on to this Truth when those around you are making you wrong and invalidating you. Remember they do this from fear of looking at themselves. When others lash out at you, it is never about you, it is about them. Yes, it sounds like it is about you and they believe it is about you, but it does not matter what they believe. What matters is what you choose to believe.

Do you choose to believe that what others say about you is who you are, or do you choose to believe the Truth that lies within you, even if you are not sure what this is in this moment? Taking a stand for Truth and for remembering who you are takes a tremendous amount of courage, especially in the face of opposition from those around you who you love and care about. We understand how desperately you want their love and support as you step out on this journey of living your authentic life and we assure you that even if you must first walk this path without physical companions, you will continue to gain strength as you take each step and you will find new companions along the path who will be delighted to support and encourage you along the way.

Remember, you can also call on non-physical beings including angels, guides, God, Jesus, Buddha, Mohamed and many others who are always there for you, no matter what, and who will always reflect the Truth back to you. You can call on your Higher Self, the part of you that already knows the Truth that has only been buried underneath the rubble. You have already connected to this part of you from time to time, even if you were unaware of it. Every time you feel happy, excited and loved, you are connected to your Higher Self, your authentic self, to God, to Source, to a Higher Power. It is in times of pain and struggle that you forget who you are and lose this connection.

You may be tempted at times to run back into the fold and hide among the others, taking comfort by their acceptance of your return, yet this comfort will be temporary. It will not be long before you will feel the inner stirring of your heart and soul calling you, once again, to step out and live YOUR life, not the life others think you should be living.

Walking the path of Truth is not easy and yet, it is the most liberating path you will find and one that leads you to all your heart's desires and to true peace, happiness and love.

Today, let's take a deeper look at one of your relationships that is causing you to suffer. It can be your relationship with your mother, father, sister, brother, spouse, friend. Choose one person to focus on for this exercise and you can repeat the exercise as many times as you like focusing on a different person each time.

Once you choose the person, think about and if possible, write down everything you believe this person believes about you. Record things they continually say about who you are, things they complain about when they verbally attack you and when you feel put down by them or hurt by them. What events do they keep bringing up from the past with accusations of things you did and what you should have done differently? Dig deep and record everything.

Here are some examples of things you may have heard them say:

* You are so selfish.

* You only think about yourself.

* Why do you always _____?

* You never _____.

* You shouldn't _____.

* If you cared you would _____.

* You always _____.

* You don't _____.

* You are _____.

Once you feel complete with your list and recordings of past events that this person continues to hold on to, go back and for each item on your list and for each event, put your focus on the person you wrote about. Remember, what others say to you says more about them than about you. Until now, you have been taking their words personally and allowed them to cause you pain and suffering. Now, we invite you to look at everything on your list and all the events you recorded from a new and different perspective.

Imagine that the person you have been focusing on has many unresolved wounds that are buried within them. They are not even aware of their own wounds and when they lash out at you with hurtful words and accusations; it is this part of them who is speaking, not their true, authentic, Higher Self.

Your actions and choices will often trigger the wounds in others who unconsciously react by verbally attacking you.

When you take their words personally, you will also be triggered and your wounds will come to the surface and you will experience pain and suffering. This is an opportunity for you to heal and grow, and one way to do this is to recognize that what others say to you and about you has NOTHING to do with you and EVERYTHING to do about them.

Going back to what you recorded today, re-read each statement and event as you imagine the words coming from a wounded child. Rather than taking the words personally and allowing them to cause you pain, send loving thoughts to the person who said these things to you, recognizing that if they felt happy and fulfilled in their life, they would not be saying these words to you and would not be confronted by the way you are choosing to live your life.

If this person tells you, for example, *"You are so selfish,"* what this could mean is that when they see you doing what you want and taking care of yourself, it brings up feelings of jealousy and anger within them because they haven't had the courage to do this for themselves and your actions are a reminder of this. Remember, when you stand in your power by being YOU, those who are afraid to do the same will unconsciously try to pull you back so that they will feel more comfortable. The more you can see the Truth and not take what they say personally, the less you will suffer as you continue along your path. Do your best not to take things personally and instead recognize that those who speak negatively are in pain and you can send them loving and healing energy while doing the same for yourself.

Everyone is doing the best they can.

MESSAGE #28

DO YOU BELIEVE IN "HAPPILY EVER AFTER?"

Continuing along this path of rediscovering who you are is a process, just as living your life up to this point has been a process. The only difference is that in this process you are in charge and you can determine which path you wish to take from a more conscious place. In the past, you blindly walked along, step by step, not really knowing where you were going. Many times you found yourself walking around in circles and wondering why you never seemed to get anywhere.

Well, now you are on a more conscious path, one that leads you to Truth and one that will set you free to BE YOU and to DO whatever brings you joy and to HAVE whatever you desire. Yes, we know this may sound like a fairy tale and many of you no longer believe in "happily ever after."

We are here to tell you that you CAN live a fairy tale life that is real and not just imagined, but you must first BELIEVE that you can.

If you continue to tell yourself that what you really want in life isn't possible, then it isn't. You really do hold the key to your own happiness and abundance. If you are not willing to accept this Truth, then you will go back to living your life the way you've been living it so far and you will continue to suffer. If you hold on to this Truth, you will begin to experience life in a new way, a liberating way, a way that leads to your own *"happily ever after."*

Of course, you will likely fall back into old patterns from time to time that may cause suffering or pain, however, you will no longer get stuck in this pain since your increased awareness will awaken you in those moments to the Truth so that you can choose to shift your perceptions and shift your way of thinking to better serve who you are.

Over time, your old, self-defeating patterns will fall away and you will find yourself dancing along your freedom path with a lighter step and a song in your heart, taking in all the beauty that is around you and the beauty that IS you.

Perhaps, you have already begun to experience some of this as you've gone through the process outlined in this book and, if you haven't, we encourage you to go back to the beginning of the book and complete the process again. Continue to work with the exercises presented in this book until you not only remember who you are on an intellectual level, but KNOW who you are in your heart and soul. Trust us when we tell you that you will know when you reach this place for you will feel it in every cell of your body and you will KNOW without any doubt that you are a Magnificent Being.

We invite you and encourage you to confidently and boldly step into your power, bringing more Light into the world, as you

Magnify Your Magnificence!

It has been an honor to serve you in this way and we invite you to call on us at any time as you continue along your journey for we are always here to help Light the way.

EPILOGUE

THE WORLD AWAITS YOU

The world awaits you as you step forth into your magnificence and magnify it so that your Light will shine brightly, leading the way for others to follow. No longer will you feel the need to pull back and hide who you are for you will see the beauty, not only in yourself, but in those around you. When you show up fully in your life, you give others permission to do the same. Yes, there may still be those around you who will try to pull you back into your old vision of yourself and yet, this will no longer have the same impact on you for you will see the Truth that they are acting from their own fears and limitations. You will now have compassion for them rather than anger and resentment for you will see their pain and suffering.

> *By magnifying your magnificence now, and in every moment, you will attract many who have been waiting for you to lead them toward their own magnificence.*

As you tap into your magnificence more and more, you will continue to be led along your path, allowing your destiny to unfold naturally and effortlessly, for your journey IS your destiny and how you experience this journey is of your own creation.

There is no right or wrong thing to do, and no right or wrong thing to BE. There is what there is and, if you are not pleased with what is, then you have the power within you to change it by creating something new.

You have been given many tools throughout this book that you can continue to use throughout your life as you uncover more and more layers of who you are not. The end of this book does not mark the end of your journey, for you have simply stepped on a new path filled with unlimited possibilities and opportunities for you to choose from. Continue to listen to what is in your heart and let this guide you as you continue along this path. When you are faced with what may appear to be an obstacle, look deeper within yourself to see the beauty of what is before you, to see the blessing and allow this perceived obstacle to be an opportunity for you to connect more deeply to your Truth and your soul's calling. When you come to a fork in the road, take time to look within before choosing which way to go. Do not be tempted or blinded by the external illusions of what you think is before you. Listen to your heart, for it will never lead you astray.

If at any time you find yourself lost, there is no need to fear. Not only can you use your ability to tap into your inner compass, you can also call on us and your guides in the higher realms to help you find your way back.

You were born to live a full and abundant life filled with love, joy and blessings. You were born to experience wonder, awe and gratitude for all that is possible. You were born to authentically express yourself and your heart's desires through your co-creations. You were born to BE YOU and to Magnify Your Magnificence so that your Light will join the Light of others transforming your world from darkness into Pure Light.

We thank you for answering *"YES"* to the call within your soul and for being such an important part of this evolutionary process. You matter. Your Light matters. You make a difference simply by being YOU!

Many Blessings Dear One

ABOUT THE AUTHOR

Marisa has often been described as loving, compassionate and non-judgmental. She understands the pain of experiencing ongoing family drama and conflict that causes separation and/or alienation between family members.

Over the course of 40+ years working on herself and learning how to love herself, Marisa was able to heal from her past wounds that were stopping her from authentically expressing herself. She now enjoys the loving and healthy relationships she always desired.

Marisa's greatest joy is empowering heart-centered women to create healthy boundaries and more harmonious family relationships. She coaches and mentors with the intuitive understanding that life's greatest challenges can be the catalyst that leads us to our greatest joy.

Through a powerful, step-by-step process, she helps women break free from their fears and the negative family patterns that keep them from authentically expressing themselves and that trap them into saying YES to others and No to themselves.

Marisa is well known for following her heart and inspiring and encouraging others to do the same. Her faith and trust in listening to and following her inner guidance led her to attract the love of her life and build her dream life in the beautiful country of Colombia, South America.

CONNECT WITH MARISA

FACEBOOK: MarisaFerrera.com/facebook

INSTAGRAM: MarisaFerrera.com/IG

TWITTER: MarisaFerrera.com/twitter

BLOG: MarisaFerrera.com/blog

YOUTUBE: MarisaFerrera.com/youtube

LINKEDIN: MarisaFerrera.com/linkedin

You can learn more about Marisa and how she can help you by visiting her website at:

MarisaFerrera.com

SPECIAL BONUS

**If you haven't already done so, I invite
you to request your Special Bonus Gift**

Now that you've completed reading the book, you can see that
each message is accompanied by a powerful exercise to support
you in integrating the message. You may find yourself drawn to
repeating some of the exercises. To make it more convenient for
you, I created a separate guide containing only the exercises,
presented in a step-by-step format.

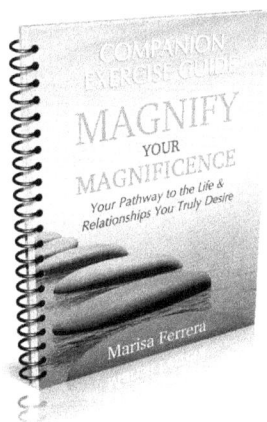

In addition to the bonus mentioned above,
I also have a surprise gift for you.

Claim Your Bonus Gifts Today!
MarisaFerrera.com/mymbonus

*You've come this far. Don't let fear or uncertainty,
or any other block, stop you from having the life
and relationships you want and deserve.
You're only a click away.*

www.ingramcontent.com/pod-product-compliance
Lightning Source LLC
LaVergne TN
LVHW051641080426
835511LV00016B/2420